WILLIAM SCHEREMET

DEAR 20 YEAR OLD ME

Everything I Wish I Knew About Relationships at Your Age

MOVING A MOUNTAIN

Dear 20 Year Old Me: Everything I Wish I Knew About Relationships at Your Age

Copyright © 2023 by William Scheremet

All rights reserved.

No part of this book may be reproduced in any form or by any electronic or mechanical means, including information storage and retrieval systems, without written permission from the author, except for the use of brief quotations in a book review.

Unless otherwise indicated, Scripture quotations are from the ESV Bible (The Holy Bible, English Standard Version) copyright © 2001 by Crossway.

Paperback ISBN: 979-8-9880685-0-1
E-book ISBN: 979-8-9880685-1-8

Contact William by email at william@movingamountain.com

www.movingamountain.com

Dedicated to the glory of Yah.

"So, whether you eat or drink, or whatever you do, do all to the glory of God."
1 Corinthians 10:31

TABLE OF CONTENTS

PROLOGUE

Sow a thought and you reap an action; Sow an act
and you reap a habit; sow a habit and you reap a
character; Sow a character and you reap a destiny.

- Ralph Waldo Emerson

If I had known how massive an impact the decisions I
made in my late teens and early twenties would have on where I
am today, I would have done things much differently. Honestly,
it would have been good to know this information even earlier
than that, but right around twenty years old is when things
really started getting out of control. Even little decisions can

ripple through the years into dramatic consequences later in life. It's like the ship that gets one degree off course at the beginning of its voyage. If it doesn't correct, it ends up miles and miles from its intended destination. The choices we make matter.

On the surface, this book is a practical guide about how to form good relationships and get better at social interaction. In a deeper sense, it's about making good decisions. If I would have known the information contained in this book back when I was 20 years old, my life may have turned out much differently. I've gotten to a place where I'm pretty happy at this point. Still, I wonder what my life could have been like if I wouldn't have made so many poor decisions earlier on. Let me give you some examples.

One late afternoon, my friend Jake and I decided to try out urban mountain biking. We went normal mountain biking in the woods pretty often, but we were stuck in the middle of the city on this particular afternoon. We decided to take our bikes and hit the University of Minnesota campus to see if there was anything that could give us the feel of real mountain biking. At first we just messed around riding over small steps and cruising down ramps. Then I saw it, a stone bench that was about 25 feet long and about two feet off the ground. I got the bright idea of riding down the bench to get some speed and then bunny hopping sideways off of it. For some reason, I didn't tell Jake what I was about to try. Perhaps, he would have talked some sense into me. There's a lesson on seeking counsel before making decisions. Regardless, I lifted my bike up on the bench, estimated how much speed I'd need, and started pedaling. The second my front tire left the bench, I knew I had made a mistake. A moment later, my face hit the pavement and someone from a group of prospective students visiting the campus yelled an expletive as he witnessed me crash. My face was in agony. My nose was broken and I was bleeding heavily. Man, I wish I had worn a helmet before attempting this stunt. There's another lesson. When I stood up, I looked at the bench and realized there were these metal plates sticking up about a half inch out of it, every few feet. They were there to prevent skateboarders from doing tricks on the bench. My mind wasn't processing things very well at the time, but later I realized my front tire had hit one of these plates right as I was launching off, causing me to flip over the handlebars and nose dive into the concrete. Thankfully, I walked away without any serious brain damage, but the fall still left a permanent reminder. My nose healed back crooked and I have a scar on my upper lip. A series of bad decisions led to a crash that permanently disfigured a part of my face. It's nothing horrible. I'm still a good looking guy. I just wanted to illustrate how little decisions can lead to major consequences and how it only takes a brief moment for your life to change permanently.

This also wasn't the worst or the only poor decision I made around that time. My life was a whole cacophony of them. Let's take money for example. I worked a lot in my late teens and early twenties, so I made a decent amount of income. Instead of saving any of it, I blew it on useless entertainment, eating out at fast food restaurants, and drugs and alcohol. The amount of money I spent on drugs and alcohol alone is mind blowing. There were times where I was probably blowing around $800/month on mind-altering substances, not to mention all the ways I threw money away due to being intoxicated. If I would have invested that money, I would probably have tens of thousands of extra dollars in the bank, without even factoring in interest or opportunity cost.

There were also many poor decisions regarding time. The number of hours sunk into video games and mindless entertainment was astronomical. I basically did the bare minimum required to get through school, and spent the rest of my time in pleasure seeking hedonism. I got good grades, but that is an incredibly low bar to hit. What could I have accomplished if I hadn't wasted so many hours on pointless nonsense? It didn't even have to be something super productive. What if instead of playing sports on a video game console, I actually went and practiced a sport in real life? I had potential in hockey. Perhaps, I would have actually gotten good if I had practiced more. Perhaps, I could have picked up a musical instrument. The possibilities are endless.

Then there were my poor decisions regarding relationships, which I must mention since that is the theme of this book. The lifestyle I lived lent itself to dysfunctional relationships. For years I totally rejected my family. I didn't want them judging my behavior, so I simply abandoned them. The people I spent my time with were the people I partied with. Some of them were decent friends, but weren't necessarily good influences on the way I lived my life. When it came to romantic relationships, that was also a mess. I was extremely anxious around girls. Instead of learning how to interact with them properly, I just numbed my anxiety by getting intoxicated. The problem with this was that I was unable to develop anything lasting or meaningful and often ended up hooking up with girls who were as much of a mess as I was. There were a few times I had the opportunity to date high quality women, and I threw them away because I didn't know what to do. If I had made better decisions, I might be married or have kids by now, and I don't even know if it's possible for me to have kids anymore because of my spinal cord injury, which brings me to the worst decision I ever made. I decided to test my limits on a dirtbike after not having ridden one for over a year. I crashed after attempting a jump, and another rider crashed into me, leaving me permanently paralyzed and totally upheaving my life and the lives of my family. That one was on another level. In an instant everything changed. I'm fortunate to even be alive.

As you can hopefully learn from my life, the choices we make today impact the place we end up tomorrow. If I could give my younger self some advice, I would tell him to do things today that the older version of himself would thank him for. Really, I would give that advice to anyone. It's something I often try to remind myself of, and it's helped me in numerous situations. Nowadays, whenever I desire to do something I know isn't good for me, I think about what it could mean for my future. I ask myself, "Will this put me in a better spot later on?" Sometimes it is ok to take risks, but often, I think about what I'm about to do and realize I should do something else.

Our modern world is steeped in instant gratification. We expect things at an ever accelerating rate. This makes it easy to fall into the trap of seeking short term pleasure at the cost of losing long term fulfillment. The internet and technology only compound this effect. Young people are growing up in a world full of temptations towards bad decision making. Instead of learning, they ask Google. Instead of cooking a meal, they eat fast food garbage. Instead of marriage and family, they seek hookups and independence. Young people often don't realize what they're sacrificing by the decisions they make. Through this book, I hope to inspire at least a few of them to consider the choices they make, so that they can set themselves up for success. Do something today that your future self will thank you for.

INTRODUCTION

When I first started writing this book, I wasn't intending for it to be a book at all. It was originally going to be a video course. As a filmmaker that is usually the first medium I go to when I want to communicate an idea. However, as the idea developed I realized that part of the problem young people have with social skills is due to being on a screen too much. Soon after this realization, I lost the conviction to make a video course. Relationships are something that happen in person. You need to be able to see the microexpressions on someone's face or feel the soft touch of someone trying to comfort you. Though the internet and social media have made lofty promises of greater connection, they have fallen dramatically short. People, especially young people, feel more isolated, anxious, and depressed than ever before. Relationships and screens are like oil and water. They don't mix. For that reason I decided not to continue with the video course. However, I had already begun writing a script and I still wanted to communicate this information somehow. I wasn't exactly sure what that would look like, but I kept writing. This book is the result of me trying to get my thoughts organized and down on paper. I hope that it will turn into a live event someday so that people can learn about relationships while experiencing the real life interaction I envision, but for now this book seems like a good way to start.

It took a couple of months for the inspiration for this project to develop. The initial idea came when I was working with kids and teenagers as a cognitive trainer, spending many hours getting to know them personally. I started noticing a lot of patterns in their thinking and behavior regarding relationships, and I realized that many of these young people weren't getting taught how to interact with other people properly. I saw teenage girls being hyper sexualized, and believing they were only valuable for their bodies. I had teenage guys tell me about hooking up with multiple girls in one night. I saw elementary school aged kids being shown confusing information about gender and identity, some even living out their lives as the opposite sex. These are things I noticed when I worked as a missionary on college campuses as well. It was like everyone just assumed that kids would be alright. They would just pick up their social skills naturally through interacting with other kids as they grew up.

There didn't seem to be any kind of focused education on how to relate to other people. Sure, socialization through experience is a major piece of the puzzle, but if that is the only thing utilized, it presents some potential pitfalls. For example, what happens when a child is put into a dysfunctional social situation such as being surrounded by bullies with no one to help? That's a situation I faced personally, and it caused tremendous problems for me with ramifications lasting into adulthood. I have dealt with major trust issues, anxiety, and self-reliance. When I enter a confrontational situation, it can feel like I am unsafe because when I was bullied there was no one there to help me, and it feels the same now, even when I know that's not the case. That has led to avoiding confrontation, which leaves issues unresolved and repressed, and that is just one of the challenges I've had to overcome. Socialization through experience alone doesn't always work.

I began to think about what might have helped me when I was 20 years old. I see real life social situations more like an ice arena on game day. If you threw a random guy who has never even seen a pair of skates into a hockey game, you can imagine how that might go. Now imagine that a whole bunch of people with zero knowledge and zero experience with hockey are thrown on a rink and told to play a game with each other. Would you expect it to look anything even like a hockey game? How long would it take them to figure it out? If people need to know the rules and fundamental techniques before they can play a simple game of hockey well, why would we assume that people don't need to be taught social skills before they can engage in relationships well?

It saddened me to see these kids I was working with struggle with relationships and unhealthy behavior. I knew the stuff they told me would likely lead to painful situations for them because that's what happened in my own life, and it's what I've seen happen over and over again to people exhibiting similar behavior. I learned a lot of lessons regarding relationships the hard way. Just like what I was seeing with these kids, when I was growing up I didn't learn how to interact with people very well. Sure, I had friends to play with as a kid and my parents taught me things like how to be polite and respectful, but it was all pretty shallow. No one ever sat me down and showed me the fundamentals of human relationships. On top of that, I didn't have many healthy relationships modeled for me. My parents loved me and taught me a lot of things, but they also fought all the time and eventually got divorced.

Like many kids nowadays, I was also exposed to pornography at around the age of 9 or 10, and became addicted soon after. Pornography presents an extremely perverted form of relationships that has nothing to do with love. It is solely focused on pleasure and using other people, and that is the exact perspective that infected my thinking. Those are just a couple of the examples I had for learning how relationships work, but you can start to see how it may have led to a distorted understanding of things like love and sexuality.

When I was 11 years old my family moved, and I started going to a new school. For all of middle school I was severely bullied, and I began to think that I was broken and worthless. After I broke my legs in a motocross accident I actually took on the nickname "Broken Bill." It matched the physical reality of my injury, but it also encapsulated how I thought of myself.

The nickname stuck. When I was 12 years old I began drinking alcohol, and I don't mean just sneaking a couple sips from my uncle's beer. I'm talking full blown binge drinking. I realized that when I drank I would get bullied less, and I got the added reward of feeling the fun effects of alcohol. This began conditioning me to think that my value was based on how messed up on alcohol and drugs I could get.

For the next 13 years I thought that being belligerent was the best way to make friends, and getting high was how to live the best life. All of this stuff made for a whirlwind of dysfunctional and broken relationships. At this point you might be thinking, "How in the world does this qualify someone to talk about relationships?" Don't worry, the story isn't finished yet.

When I was 25 years old I broke my back in another motocross accident and became paralyzed from the belly down. My entire life was turned upside down. I had everything stripped away from me and I had to rediscover who I was and what purpose I had. This led me on a long journey of truth seeking, about the way the world worked and about myself. At 26, I encountered Jesus Christ and developed a relationship with God, which was the most healing thing that has ever happened to me. I also did a lot of deep diving into my past and worked through the different traumas I suffered. I forgave people. I sought out the lies and faulty belief systems I held and replaced them with truth. I made new friends, ones who cared about me in both good and bad situations. I also studied psychology and social interaction often.

At this point my confidence is more solid than it has ever

been, even though I use a wheelchair and am limited in a lot of ways I haven't been in the past. Despite what others think, I can honestly say that I feel comfortable being myself, and I have developed many meaningful relationships. Now that you know that part of my story, hopefully you can see that I have a unique perspective when it comes to approaching this stuff. I'm someone who had to get here through a lot of trial and error. I had to work for it. I had to overcome obstacles. It might have taken me a longer time to arrive, but I went a lot deeper as well. Not only do I have the knowledge and life experience, but I am living evidence that even the worst case scenario can be turned around. If I can come from the background I came from and learn how to have trustful meaningful relationships, anyone can. It's not just for those who came from good homes with loving families and childhood friends that stuck with them their entire lives. Drug addicts, orphans, and delinquents can turn things around too. It will take the grace of God, and some effort on your part, but it will be worth it. And even if you didn't come from a rough background, you can still learn from this book. These concepts apply to everyone. This is all the information I wish I would have had when I was 20 years old, though I could have used it at almost any time in my life. These are very human ideas and there is enough material to go deep on many of them. It will take time and effort if you truly want to change your life, but again, it's well worth it.

There are many people out there teaching things that might help you become more attractive or successful, but often by means that will also make you more selfish and manipulative.

They won't lead to happiness or fulfillment in your life. They won't give you rock solid confidence that allows you to feel good about yourself. Many people will try to make you think that it is not even possible to be a kind, honest, and loving person and still be attractive. That's a total lie. It's possible to be both a good person and attractive. In fact, it will actually make you more attractive to the right type of people, those who are going to care for and support you in all circumstances, not just when you're successful. And it will make you feel good about yourself because you will know that it's not a cheap gimmick or artificial technique that has made you attractive and successful in relationships. It will come from being authentic and honest. This isn't just about doing something to get a certain result. Don't get me wrong, I want you to see results. However, this is about becoming a better person, someone of value and integrity who will naturally be attractive to others. My goal is to equip you with good and truthful information that will help you spot the lies and temptations the world presents you, and help you to make good decisions that will lead to healthy relationships and greater fulfillment in all aspects of your life.

So what can you expect from this material? There is going to be a lot of info about romantic relationships, but they aren't the only relationships talked about. The ideas contained here can be applied to many different relational situations. Maybe you have only made friends through your social circles in the past. It's good to have those relationships, but what if the people in your social circles don't hold the same values as you or aren't motivated towards the same goals you are?

The people surrounding you aren't always going to be people who want the same things you do. They might have different political opinions, they might be into partying all the time, or they might simply not have the same level of ambition and creativity as you. That would mean you are missing out on relationships with people who could really enhance your quality of life. If you implement what is in this book, you will likely be able to make friends with people in many situations. You could even decide to build your own social circle, and fill it with people who share the same values as you and who you truly enjoy being around. You will learn that it is even possible to walk up to strangers and start a conversation. Maybe you are looking for a husband or a wife. If you implement what is in this book you will become more attractive and know how to navigate romantic relationships so that you can set yourself up for success and avoid heartbreak. Maybe you have a desire to grow your career or business. Knowing how to communicate is key for that. The material in this book will help you develop yourself into the type of person that people will want to work with. The enhanced social skills you learn will help you become better at networking and interviewing. Maybe you've had some rough relationships in the past. This book will teach you how to heal from trauma and learn to see your bad experiences as hidden gifts. No matter where you are in life, I hope the information in this book will be helpful in some way. Before we jump into the how of relationships, let's take a minute to reflect on why they are important.

CHAPTER 1

WHY RELATIONSHIPS?

Alright, so here you are, about to jump into a bunch of material on relationships and social interaction. You might be thinking a number of different things. "Is this worth my time? What could I possibly learn that I haven't already heard? Come on, just give me the skills I need to get a girlfriend or boyfriend already." Alright alright. I know you want to start having fulfilling relationships asap, but it's really important to look at why they matter in the first place. Without that understanding, none of the other stuff you learn will make sense, and any changes in your life will only be superficial. This isn't going to be a book you just read through as fast as you can and magically your relationships become awesome. It is going to take a lot of hard work. You need to understand why having good relationships is important because it will help you stay motivated as you work through the material. So let's begin.

First of all, humans are relational creatures. One of our primary purposes is to exist in relationships. This includes romantic relationships, but there are many others as well. There are relationships with other people, with ourselves, with God, and even with nature. There are family relationships, friendships, romantic relationships, and societal relationships. Relationships affect nearly every aspect of our lives, so it's important for us to understand them. They are where we learn, they help us deal with hardship, they give us joy, they allow us to share, and they are valuable for so many other reasons that it would be difficult to go through them all right now. The point you should take away is that relationships are extremely important!

Let me give you a little thought experiment to illustrate what I mean. Imagine you had all the money in the world. You could go anywhere, try anything, and you would never have to work another day in your life. This sounds like a pretty sweet deal, right? But imagine there's a catch; you have to give up interacting with other people altogether. Some of you might be thinking, "That doesn't sound too bad. People have been getting on my nerves lately and I could use a break." Ok, that's understandable. Sometimes it's good to get away from the chaos. You might even have fun for a little while. Maybe even a long while. But eventually you wouldn't be able to take being by yourself any longer. There would be no one to share that five star prime rib dinner with. There would be no one to tell the story about almost being eaten by a lion on your African safari to. There is a reason social media platforms have grown to epic proportions. People want to share their lives with others. I would argue that social media is a poor way of doing this, but the rise of these platforms illustrates my point, even if it is a misdirected way of seeking community.

Isolation often leads to loneliness, depression, and all kinds of horrible consequences. There is a reason why solitary confinement is considered one of the worst tortures a person can endure. Life is only good in the context of relationships. Yet, many of us don't have a clue what a healthy one looks like. Our lives are full of broken and complicated relationships. Much of the stress, anxiety, depression, and other problems in our lives stem from these relational issues. Some of us don't have any healthy relationships at all. If we are literally made for relationships, but don't have any good ones, you can imagine the problems this might cause.

So how did we get here? Well, it goes all the way back to the garden. Our first ancestors, Adam and Eve, who were the first humans, were also the first humans to experience broken relationships. I'll get into that more later, but for now it is enough to realize that this is a universal human problem. There are many places where we're supposed to learn how to have good relationships, but don't.

The first and foremost is through our families. Yes, some people have a pretty good family situation, but many of us have families that are broken, and so we don't learn about good relationships there. For example, you might have had parents that cheated on each other or siblings that betrayed you. Maybe you had family members who were cold or distant.

Maybe your parents got divorced or fought with each other all the time. Some of you might not have had parents at all. Don't worry. These things aren't uncommon. They are also not your fault. You had no control over the environment you were raised in. Still, without people to teach and model good relationships for you, you might not have learned the skills you need to have strong healthy ones now, and you might have picked up some bad habits along the way.

Ok, what about school? That's where we learn, right? Don't we learn how to socialize there? Yes, but usually not formally, and often very poorly. Kids aren't usually experts on relationships, and most teachers aren't either. There are kids who are bullies and there are teachers who rule with an iron fist. The experience you get from school might be enough to help you survive, but rarely is it going to be enough to help you thrive. And as I mentioned earlier, there usually isn't any formal teaching on relationships that you'll receive in school. The most you might get is a sex-ed class, but this is usually more focused on the biological aspects of relationships, and it often neglects all the other skills such as communication and boundary setting. It also lacks some foundational beliefs about identity and dignity that will help you to have strong fulfilling relationships and be more confident.

Ok, so without family or schooling to provide strong foundations for having good relationships, where do we go? We all want to have good relationships, so often we do our best, but this can lead to looking in many of the wrong places. We end up stumbling along, taking whatever resources we can find.

This often isn't successful, and can even be dangerous. Let's look at a few more of these other places you might turn to for information so you can get a better idea of what I'm talking about.

One place you might try to learn about relationships is through culture. If everyone else is doing something, that must mean it's the best thing to do, right? Oftentimes not, and in fact it's usually the opposite. Copying the crowd has the potential to make you less attractive, less confident, and less valuable to others. You end up becoming like everyone else, rather than becoming who you truly are. This is something I experienced in my own life. For years I tried to fit in and be what I thought other people wanted me to be. This led to alcoholism, drug addiction, sex addiction, and a bunch of other dysfunctional behavior. The things I would see in the culture were the things I tried to emulate. My friends and I got a lot of our ideas through the movies and music we consumed. Movies like Old School and Wedding Crashers taught us that life was about partying and hooking up with people. The music we listened to was often about drug use and criminal behavior. My time in college was especially culture driven. It was this strange place where a bunch of 18 to 22 year olds got together in a little cultural bubble with no parents or authority figures to watch over us. Sure, we had professors we were accountable to regarding school work, but outside of that we basically did whatever we wanted. But the more I tried to fit in, the more I lost touch with who I truly was. My true self didn't match the culture, and the farther away from myself I got, the more anxious and depressed I became. The only times I was able to interact with women was when I was drunk or high. I had no idea how to be genuine and authentic. I was just imitating others. This led to me becoming isolated, lonely, and desperate. Trying to fit in with the culture didn't work.

It's ok to imitate others in things that are good. That's how we learn. However, culture is constantly changing. It is full of trends and fashions. When you create your identity off of these things, you end up having to change just as quickly as the culture changes. The things you really want to imitate should be based on lasting truths that never change. That way, you are grounded. Culture is also one of the most dangerous places to learn about relationships. There are many lies and tons of propaganda circulating in culture.

Many of the ideas found in modern culture were birthed through advertising. People wanted to sell a product so they made it look enticing. They do this so you will buy more of their product, not because they actually care about your well-being. From there these ideas become popular and find their way into every aspect of society. This doesn't necessarily equate to good information though. For example, in order to have healthy relationships, you need to understand that you are a unique person with dignity and value, but the culture doesn't see you this way. The culture views you as an object to market things to. The culture only wants you for your utility. This utilitarian worldview ends up sending messages that often make people believe that they are not good or beautiful enough, and they actually strip away their dignity and value. Just look at some of the messages culture sends about men and women. Girls are depicted as hyper-emotional princesses, sex objects, or so strong and independent that they don't need men at all. Men are depicted as bumbling idiots or cold heartless creatures with no emotion. A more recent idea is that you don't have to be a man or a woman at all. You can choose whatever gender you want to be! These ideas all distort your sense of identity. Without knowing your identity, you can't know your purpose, and without knowing your identity, you can't have good relationships. Identity will be covered more in depth a little later, but for now just know that culture is a dangerous place to learn about relationships.

Another place you might turn to learn about relationships is the internet. There is a lot of good information on the internet, but there is probably even more bad information. You never really know what you are getting up front. It can be like searching for buried treasure to find the good stuff. Most of the things you'll find on the internet sound great, but then lead to even more dysfunction. Dating gurus will teach you how to attract someone, but they will also teach you that you have to be selfish and narcissistic to do so, or they will focus solely on the physical aspect of relationships, turning you into pleasure seeking hedonists. That kind of lifestyle will never lead you to develop healthy fulfilling relationships.

Another danger of the internet is that many of the ideas you will find are simply there because they will make someone money. With regards to relationships, salesmen and marketers know they can capitalize on all the lonely people desperate to find love. Sometimes this can include people who actually have good content, but oftentimes it is people who just threw something together that sounds good in order to make a quick buck. These things might give you some surface level results, but rarely will you find something that will create lasting change on a deep personal level. At least these types of gimmicks probably won't do much harm, besides maybe ripping you off. But, there are things out there that actually will.

About ten years ago I got caught up in a part of the internet called the Red Pill. At the time, it was mostly a place for men to learn how to attract women. At least that's how it looked on the surface. There were indeed some genuinely great ideas there and not all of this part of the internet was bad. I did learn some things that helped me become more successful in attracting women such as being less needy, working on developing myself, and taking responsibility for my life. However, I also developed some horrible perspectives. The niche part of this community I found was extremely toxic. My attitude towards women became extremely resentful and led to much worse relationships overall. The women I interacted with were often broken themselves, and any relationship I had was short lived. One time I was out at a bar and ran into this girl who started berating me. I found out she was the friend of another girl I hooked up with and then ignored. This girl was furious at the way I had treated her friend. I basically blew her off. There was still a part of me that felt a twinge of guilt, but for the most part I didn't care. I couldn't see the damage I had done. In my eyes, men and women cheated on each other, and it was just the way the world worked.

If there was any reason women liked me at all, it was

probably due to exhibiting slightly more confidence. However, I was also learning to have zero compassion or empathy. I began to believe that every woman was a lying cheater, and so that's how I treated them. Through this dark part of the internet I was in, I learned to become more and more self-centered, and I took on all kinds of relationship destroying behavior. I would even do things like try to hit on my friends' girlfriends behind their backs. One time I thought I was playing footsie with my friend's girlfriend under a table we were sitting at, and it turned out I was actually playing footsie with my friend! Let me tell you, that is not the way to build strong trusting relationships with people! You will lose all your friends, and if the person you are pursuing is willing to cheat WITH you, they will also cheat ON you. Ironically, I was taught that there are no good women out there, and that every single woman will cheat on you and betray you as soon as she finds someone better, so you had to learn to see women as dispensable right from the start. Of course it's going to seem like all women are like this if you treat them that way. It's a self-fulfilling prophecy. Your behavior will almost always attract the type of people that are suited to it. There is a section later in this book about confirmation bias that explains how this works in depth. If you act like a jerk, you're going to attract broken people who are also jerks. If you act with virtue, you will attract good people. This applies to the way women treat men as well.

Not surprisingly, the men who were involved in the Red Pill community were often bitter and had a strong hatred of women. Many of them were guys who had struggled with women throughout their lives and then found some initial success by becoming jerks. That was the identity of this community. It was toxic and extremely dangerous, especially because they proclaimed that this was the harsh truth of life, and it was the only truth. This is the type of stuff you might stumble upon by looking for answers on the internet. And that is just in regards to literal relationship advice. There are other ways we might seek to learn about relationships on the internet that are done in a more secondary way.

For example, social media is another part of the internet where you might try to learn about relationships. After all, it's meant to make us more connected, right? Unfortunately, that doesn't seem to be how it plays out. You may have even heard that social media actually makes people significantly less social and leads to increases in depression, anxiety, and other problems. This is actually something I studied when I was in college. I wrote my senior paper on Problematic Internet Use. Here is a section from that paper:

"There are many possible predictors of Problematic Internet Use that have been proposed such as shyness, loneliness, and social anxiety. (Caplan, 2007; Ceyhan & Ceyhan, 2008; Chak & Leung, 2004; Larose, Lin & Eastin, 2003; Oktan, 2011) These predictors all seem to have some connection with avoiding social interaction. A lack of social skills, a fear of social interaction, or simply a distaste for social interaction in the first place could cause people to seek out the Internet as an escape from real life interactions. The other possibility is that Internet abuse causes people to rely less on their social skills, therefore causing them social anxiety when faced with real interactions. It is likely that Internet Addiction Disorder is a two-way street where certain factors are predictors and also results of excessive Internet use."[1]

Whatever the cause, internet use and positive social interaction don't mix very well. Yet, internet use has skyrocketed. Around 45% of teens report that they use the internet "almost constantly," and another 44% report going online several times per day.[2] That's a problem because we are discovering that social media has many negative consequences. Among a sample of students from grades 7-12 in Ontario, those spending five or more hours per day on social media are significantly more likely to rate their mental health as "poor" or fair," to indicate moderate-to-serious psychological distress, and to report suicidal ideation compared with students who spend less time on social media or none at all.[3] The symptoms exhibited by problematic internet use are very similar to addictions such as substance abuse and gambling.[4]

If this is the case, why are more and more people flocking to the internet? Well, there are many possible reasons, and in reality we still don't know all that much about how social media affects us, even though it is a major part of our lives today. One thing to consider is that social media is this weird place where people only present the very best parts of their lives, or even what they perceive to be the best parts of their lives. This can lead to comparison and foster envy. It can also lead people to get better at presenting themselves in a false light. They externalize their identity onto a digital avatar rather than internalizing it and becoming grounded in who they actually are. Plus, there are certain things you just can't get through a screen. Much of the interaction we have through social media is superficial. It doesn't allow for the deep connection that we can only get in person. It doesn't allow us to get to know the whole person. At the same time, it can provide an escape that might *feel* like real social interaction, tricking users into thinking they are being social, when in reality it is being used as a way to avoid in-person social interaction. Besides that, social media is extremely addictive and can lead to some very dysfunctional and harmful behavior. Cyber bullying, for example, can really hurt people, and things like Tik-tok and Instagram can easily lead people to oversexualized content, sexual predators, or pornography.

Pornography is by far the most dangerous thing on the internet. It teaches people extreme objectification and leads to all kinds of societal consequences. It strips people of their dignity and it can even lead some into antisocial behavior. That's literally the opposite of having healthy relationships. Often it's pornography that causes people to become abusive in relationships, and it can even lead some to commit sex crimes.[5] Not only that, but it affects the brain in massive and disturbing ways. You are literally addicting yourself to sex on a primal level. One of our most basic human instincts is for sex. By using pornography, a person trains their brain using the pleasure reward system that is connected to those sexual instincts. I won't go into it too much further at this point, but just know there are serious psychological and physiological consequences to watching pornography. It can cause you to lose your ability to focus, lose your ability to get aroused, and feel a sense of shame that is impossible to shake. There will be a chapter that goes deeper into why and how this happens later in the book. In regards to what we are currently talking about, many young people are actually learning about relationships through pornography and this is causing untold amounts of harm. It presents an absolutely diabolical perversion of what healthy relationships are supposed to be.

Beyond these extreme dangers of the internet, another reason it might not be the best source for learning about relationships is that it can simply be hard to sift through all the information. There are good sources out there, but they can be hard to find, and they probably won't give you the full picture. That's one of the reasons I wrote this book. There is a dire need for understanding relationships and social interaction in today's world. Many people are suffering from loneliness, anxiety, and depression because they simply don't know how to interact with people and develop healthy relationships. At the same time, it is difficult to find good information that is truly comprehensive about this subject, while also being practical. I hope to do both. I wanted to compile all the things I've learned into one place, and provide a resource that will actually help people change and create thriving social lives that are full of deep healthy relationships. That's what this book is about. With that, it's finally time to jump into the deep!

CHAPTER 2

GETTING STARTED

At this point, you might be thinking, "Ok, so now can you show me what to do so I can get a girlfriend or boyfriend already?" Don't worry. There are specific actions you can take to make yourself more attractive, and we will get to that, but keep in mind, that is only a small part of the equation.

Sure, you could skip ahead to the practical skills and you would see some results pretty much as quickly as you could implement them, but ultimatel your relationships would still not be the fulfilling and joyful ones we are going for here.

If I had to give an estimate, about 80% of having successful relationships comes from having a strong sense of identity and understanding some foundational principles I am going to lay out for you. The other 20% comes from the external practical skills such as body language and how you present yourself. The ratio might even be closer to 90/10%. What I'm getting at is that you could have all the external skills mastered, but if you don't understand the foundational principles or have a strong sense of identity, your relationships will still fail.

On the other hand, if you do have a strong sense of identity and understand the foundational principles of good relationships, you could be awful at the external skills and still have great fulfilling relationships. That's why starting with this foundational material is super important. As I stated earlier, this is about you becoming a better person, a person of honesty and integrity, and someone who is confident in themself. Your relationships should enhance your life and the lives of others around you, and should not become dysfunctional or destructive.

The people who are going to get the most out of this book are those who take the time to go through the entire thing and really integrate the material into their lives. So as we begin, keep that in mind. Do you want to take the easy route that will only mildly help your communication skills, or do you want to take the time to learn and apply what is here so that your life is totally transformed? Do you want relationships where you are constantly in fear of abandonment and betrayal, or relationships where you can feel free to be yourself and trust other people? I hope that you will see the value in what you're about to learn. There's going to be a treasure chest of wisdom here.

CHAPTER 3

FOUNDATIONS

You are made to love, and love is a great thing, but it's important to understand what love truly is. We want to get it right. Often we receive a distorted view of love. The world likes to present us with all kinds of different things and call them love. Maybe it's a romantic comedy that presents obsession as love, or maybe it's a commercial for ice cream which uses seductive language to present pleasure in food as love. There are so many distorted ideas about love out there. Love is more than just an emotion. It's a gift of self. It's a choice to want and work for the best for someone else, regardless of how difficult. Love is a free and total gift. It does not withhold itself. It does not come with conditions. It risks its own safety for the good of others. Making this gift of love should bring life to the world. We are wired with the desire to love and to be loved. Again, this is a good thing. However, it needs to be directed towards life. The desire for love should propel us to do what is good and life-giving for others, whether physically, emotionally, or spiritually. Love upholds our dignity and the dignity of those around us. It's not selfish. Love does not use or abuse others. Love is about finding what's good in others and seeking to bring out more of it.

The first thing you need to understand if you want to have good relationships is that the way you perceive and express yourself is extremely important. People will reflect who you are back to you, so if you want relationships with people who are loving and authentic, you need to be loving and authentic. Success in relationships is more about what is happening in you internally than it is about external circumstances. When you come from a place where you are solid in your identity and are able to express yourself honestly, you will naturally be attractive to people because we all desire that kind of confidence and authenticity. So with that, I want to first let you know that you are a unique, unrepeatable person with dignity and value, and so are the others around you. We are all made in the image of God. You are here for a reason. You are important. You have a unique gift to offer the world. You are not defined by your struggles or your flaws. You are not just a collection of body parts. You are a whole person. You are not simply an animal driven by instinct. You have a rational mind and are able to make choices. That means those choices matter. The way you treat yourself and others matters. It will affect your life and the lives of those around you.

I know this all probably sounds a little lofty right now, but it's vital to have this understanding before you enter into relationships. It's essential because it will help you make choices that are generous rather than selfish. You need to see that relationships are not about getting pleasure for yourself. They are about sharing, and helping others to become better people. If you don't understand this, your relationships will likely become relationships of use and maybe even abuse. This can lead to emotional problems and all kinds of destructive behavior. It can leave you feeling empty and worthless. I don't want that for you because I know how painful it is. You should be able to experience joy and fulfillment in your relationships. You should be able to understand your purpose in life and to be totally content with who you are as a person. Your life is important. It's important to me, it's important to God, and it should be important to you. When you see everyone as someone with value, you treasure them. You want to protect and uphold them. You actually desire what is best for them. This will lead you to become a person of integrity and virtue, a person that does what's right no matter the cost because you recognize the importance of every human life. If you're here for selfish reasons, you've come to the wrong place. The world doesn't need more arrogant and selfish people. It needs people of integrity who will love with their whole lives. If you've read this far, and this sounds like the kind of life you want to live, keep reading. It's only going to get better.

CHAPTER 4

WHAT DOES A GOOD RELATIONSHIP LOOK LIKE?

Let's start with what a good relationship looks like. There are some things here that are going to be controversial, but you need to be presented with the truth as it is. Some people aren't going to like it, but that's usually the case when truth is presented. It's also a good lesson to learn. People won't always agree with you and they won't always like you. The sooner you become ok with that, the sooner you will be able to live your life with purpose. Here I want to reiterate what true love is. It's a free gift of self, that desires the good of others, regardless of the consequences. There are things I could tell you that would make you feel good, but telling you the truth is what's going to actually help you. It's like the doctor who has to cut you open to remove the tumor in your lungs. He could give you a pain killer that makes you feel better, but in order to actually save your life he has to cut you open. So with that being said, let me drop the first truth bomb, this one being about romantic relationships. They are meant to be between one man and one woman.

I can practically feel some of you squirm at that statement, but that's what's true. You can tell just by looking at men's and women's bodies. Men and women have different parts and they only work together when there is one of each. Remember how we said love is life-giving? Well, the highest form of that we have is the conception of new life through the coming together of one man and one woman through sex. Sex is so life-giving that it actually produces new humans. You can't get that with a man and a man or a woman and a woman. Imagine having a choice between three different seatbelts. One has a male and a female connector, one has two female connectors, and the final one has two male connectors. If you choose any seatbelt combination besides the first one, the seatbelt wouldn't work and your life would be at risk. It's the same with romantic relationships. They will only work and bear fruit if you have a man and a woman. Even if that makes sense to you, why just one man and one woman? There are a few reasons. A major one is for the protection of the children who are conceived. Every child deserves to have both a mother and a father, and to have a mother and a father who stick together. Statistically we know that children who have both a mother and a father do significantly better in life than those who don't.[6] It might seem like we are getting a little ahead of ourselves here by discussing marriage and parenting. However, my next point will help you understand why it's important to understand this stuff.

There is an end in mind

A principle of good romantic relationships is that there is an end in mind. Dating is not just a means of having fun. It's meant to help you figure out if you want to marry someone or not. Marriage is the ultimate goal of any romantic relationship. It is the highest form of commitment two people can make, and there are a ton of reasons why it is beneficial. It establishes a foundation of trust, it protects the emotional bonds which are created through sex, and it provides a safe environment for children to flourish. There is no higher relationship that can occur between humans, therefore it is the logical goal of romantic relationships.

Dating isn't simply a recreational activity. There is supposed to be a purpose to it. It's supposed to be a period of time where you see if the other person possesses virtue and if there is chemistry between you. This doesn't mean that the first person you date can't be a good match, but often it takes some trial and error to figure out who is right for you. It is ok to date multiple people. Just recognize that at some point you should intend to make a commitment to one of them. Also, I'm not telling you to become a player who keeps multiple girlfriends or boyfriends hanging around. What I'm saying is that it's ok to try going out with different people so you can get a better understanding of what you like and don't like and who might be a good match for you.

So what are some good qualities to look for in a mate? Men often value beauty. Women often value status or money. I'm not going to say these things don't matter because they are important to take into consideration. However, they aren't the most important things. Not even close actually. The emphasis that is put on these qualities in our modern culture is extremely exaggerated, and it is leading to a lot of dysfunctional relationships. For example, you can have a beautiful wife, but if she ends up cheating on you and stealing your kids, you are going to regret marrying her. Suddenly, you are on your own, paying child support, and utterly heartbroken. Women, you could find a rich husband, but maybe he doesn't listen to you and is gone all the time. You will be equally unhappy. There are multiple things to consider, and the most important ones involve a person's character. Is this person caring? Are they humble enough to admit when they are wrong? Do they share the same political and religious beliefs as you? Can you rely on them? Are they trustworthy? How do they treat their friends and family? How do they treat strangers? These are the kinds of questions you should be asking. Compatibility shouldn't be determined purely on the basis of emotion or desire. Just because it "feels" right to be with someone doesn't mean that it is. You have to use both your mind and your heart to determine whether someone is right for you. This is one of the reasons it's good to refrain from physical intimacy at the beginning of a relationship. "Wait, what did he just say!?" Bear with me. I know this probably goes against everything you've heard and everything you feel. Suspend your suspicions for just a little while so I can make my case.

When you engage in physical intimacy it creates emotional bonds between you and the other person, even with something as small as a hug or holding hands.[7] When your emotions get involved too early, it can be hard to think clearly about whether the other person is good for you or not. You become blinded by emotion. Therefore it's an important responsibility for you not to lead people on or play with their emotions. Detachment in relationships will help you judge the other person's character better. It will also make them feel more comfortable around you. One thing that can be extremely unattractive is neediness. It puts a lot of pressure on people, and most people usually don't like having pressure put on them in that way. Take it easy at the beginning. This will help you avoid neediness and discern with a clear mind.

Another question you should ask when thinking about romantic relationships is, can I sacrifice my own desires so that the other person gets what's best for them? Remember that relationships are about giving freely. If you create emotional bonds with someone by engaging in physical intimacy and then it doesn't work out, those emotional bonds break and it causes wounding. If you risk wounding someone by engaging in physical intimacy, do you really think that's doing what's best for them? If you are able to sacrifice your desire for physical intimacy, it shows the other person that you really care about them and want to protect them. A good question to ask yourself is, "Do I respect this person enough to wait to jump into bed with them?"

Only someone who wants to use you will claim that you don't care about them unless you engage with them physically. Being able to delay gratification is a good sign that you are on the right track. If someone is unwilling to respect your boundaries with physical intimacy and they pressure you over it, that could be a clear sign that they aren't a good match for you. Often people will even use this as a way to manipulate you into getting what they want, but as soon as they get it, they're gone. If they really desire to be with you, they will wait. They should be willing to commit to you before getting physical.

Another thing to mention here is that if you care about someone, you should also want to protect their dignity and reputation. By engaging in physical intimacy too early, you could be doing serious damage to the other person's dignity and reputation. Also, as you may have noticed, I have only been suggesting not to engage in physical intimacy at the beginning of a relationship. That means that there is indeed a time when you will be able to safely get physical with someone. This isn't a course on how to avoid sex at all costs. There's a joke that goes, "Sex is awful, horrible, and disgusting, so you should save it for the person you love the most." This is often what people think of when they hear the word "chastity" or are told that they should avoid engaging in physical intimacy. This is not what I am teaching! Sex is one of the greatest gifts we've been given. The reason I'm telling you not to go down that route right away is because sex is special and shouldn't be given to just anyone. It's made for the person you commit your entire life to in marriage. If you give someone your body through sex, but haven't given your life to them in marriage, you are basically telling a lie with your body. It's our responsibility to protect each other's dignity and sexuality. Remember that you are a unique and unrepeatable person made in the image of God. You have value and dignity. You have a unique personal gift to give to the world, and part of that gift is your sexuality. It cheapens the gift if it is made easy to obtain. Therefore, it is very important to protect and honor that gift, both in ourselves and others, by saving it for the appropriate time, which is marriage.

Again, remember that emotional bonds are created through physical intimacy. Can you guess what creates the strongest bonds? Yes, the strongest ones are the ones created by having sex. That means that if you break those bonds, the biggest wounds are also inflicted. Marriage is a protection against that kind of wounding. In marriage you are free to give your body to someone because they have vowed to remain with you. You can trust that the emotional bonds you create through sex won't be broken. One note here; don't worry if you have already engaged in sexual activity. It doesn't mean that YOU are broken, that things are hopeless, or that it's too late for you. I know because I've gone through this process. Yes, virginity is a great thing, but it's not the most important thing. You certainly shouldn't take it for granted, but you also shouldn't obsess over it. You are more than just your virginity. You might have to go through some healing, which is sometimes painful, but it's possible to change and live out the things you are learning here. It is still possible to have good fulfilling relationships. Also, on the other end of the spectrum, if you are a virgin, it is nothing to be embarrassed about. There is a lot of pressure out there to lose your virginity. Especially among young men, it can be looked at as a sign of weakness if you haven't lost your virginity. In reality, it is a sign of strength and integrity, as long as you understand you are the one making the choice. You are showing that you value yourself and won't settle for less than what you're worth. Besides, sex with strangers or people you don't care about is just plain bad. Without love and care for the other person, it lacks the depth that is possible. The physical act of sex is the easy part. Giving yourself entirely, emotionally, physically, and spiritually is a much greater act. It will require more of you to wait until all of those things come together in one person you commit yourself to, but it is well worth the effort. Easy sex is going to let you down. Peer pressure is a horrible reason to give up your virginity. Anyone that looks down on you for being a virgin probably doesn't really care about you anyways. This brings me to the next important principle for having healthy relationships, boundaries.

CHAPTER 5

BOUNDARIES

Boundaries are limits placed on something in order to protect it. They act as filters. Not engaging in physical intimacy is just one of many types of boundaries. An example of a very clear physical boundary would be a fence around someone's yard. It keeps certain things in and certain things out, filtering what passes through. Another physical boundary is our skin. It keeps our blood and organs inside, while keeping dirt and germs out. There are other types of boundaries as well. There are emotional boundaries, spiritual boundaries, and boundaries on things like time or energy. For our purposes, we are going to focus on boundaries that are involved in relationships.

First, let's talk about why boundaries are important. As stated earlier, boundaries are meant to protect things. So far I have talked a lot about the importance of protecting your dignity and value as well as the dignity and value of others. One of the main ways to do this is by establishing good boundaries. Without good boundaries, you put yourself at risk of being used. You might be thinking, "But I thought you said we are supposed to offer ourselves totally and freely." That's true, but it is meant to happen in a certain context. Here is an example to show you what I mean. Imagine you are driving down the highway. In the middle and on the sides of the road there are white and yellow lines indicating where your lane is. These are boundaries. Imagine these lines didn't exist and people were able to drive however they wanted. There would be total carnage and no one would be able to drive safely. The white and yellow lines provide boundaries that allow us to drive safely and freely travel wherever we want. They aren't restricting your ability to drive. They are actually empowering you to travel quickly and effectively. This is what good boundaries do. They protect, empower, and provide freedom. The same goes for boundaries in relationships. They are necessary to protect you and anyone you are in a relationship with, and they give you freedom to enjoy the relationship.

Boundaries are also highly attractive. It might seem like saying "no" to people would push them away, but actually it is the opposite. Boundaries signal to others that you value yourself, and if you value yourself people will assume that you are actually valuable. Think of going to a football game and sitting in the VIP section. This section is usually pretty expensive to sit in. One of the reasons for that is that not just anyone can come in. People value it for its exclusivity. That's what happens when you set and maintain boundaries. Have you ever noticed how attractive people sometimes play hard to get? Often it's unintentional, but sometimes people will literally try to make it hard for others to connect with them for the purpose of making themselves more attractive. Now I'm not suggesting you play games like this. I just want to illustrate this point. One of the reasons people who play hard to get are attractive is because not just anyone can have them. They make you work for it, and when you work for something you tend to value it more. For example, what would be more valuable to you, something you got for free or something you spent tons of time, energy, and money to get? You are much more likely to value the thing that cost you something over the thing that was free.

This may seem extreme, but look at women who are very promiscuous. They are a harsh example of what happens when you give something away too easily. Both men and women alike look down on them, and there have been all kinds of nasty names they've been given. Women dislike them because it puts more pressure on themselves to be promiscuous, and men will use them for sex but simultaneously despise them for giving something so precious away. One of the main things men value in a woman is purity. Our modern culture might try to make people believe otherwise, imposing the idea that men just want easy sex, but on a biological level, men actually desire chaste women. The reason is due to the reproductive nature of male and female sexuality. If a woman has sex with multiple men in a short period of time and gets pregnant, there is no way to know who the father is. We have DNA paternity tests now, but that is a recent invention. Human sexuality didn't develop under those conditions. Historically, men who chose a promiscuous mate had a higher likelihood of raising a child who wasn't theirs, and this still happens all the time today. This isn't meant to demean promiscuous women, or to excuse promiscuity in men. Morally, it is just as repugnant for men to be promiscuous as women. I'm simply trying to point out what happens when something valuable is given away too easily. This doesn't mean women who have been promiscuous are doomed to an undesirable fate. If they change their behavior, their strength will return and their worth will increase in the eyes of men and women alike. The point is that things that are easy to get are less attractive than things that take effort to obtain.

Thankfully, you don't have to play games to become attractive. You can achieve this same effect by maintaining good boundaries. These will naturally make you hard to get without having to pretend. You shouldn't say no to people just to make it hard for them. If you develop good boundaries all you have to do is maintain them. In order to maintain boundaries, you will have to say no to certain things and this inevitably will make you hard to get. So what are some good examples of relational boundaries?

Well, I already mentioned not engaging in physical intimacy, but I want to emphasize this again in the context of boundaries. By setting a limit on how far you are going to go physically with someone, you do a few things. First, you protect your dignity and the dignity of the person you are in the relationship with. Remember that one of the functions of boundaries is to protect things. Here, you also protect yourselves from breaking the emotional bonds that are created through physical intimacy. I have already talked about those things, but there's even more. By not engaging in physical intimacy right away, you leave room for growth in other parts of the relationship. You get to figure out things you like doing together, what kinds of conversations interest you, and how you relate to each other's friends, for example. There is less pressure on you to please the other person physically or to do something you aren't comfortable with. When you set very clear boundaries such as "we aren't going to kiss until we are in an exclusive committed relationship," it gives you a clear guide for knowing how far is too far. It is important to establish these boundaries ahead of time, because trying to limit yourself in a moment of temptation is not going to work. Setting limits on physical intimacy will also protect you from unexpected pregnancies and sexually transmitted diseases. One final reason to think about boundaries on physical intimacy is that if you get married someday, you will be able to give your spouse a gift that only they get to experience. This will be very special to them and will strengthen your marriage immensely. Again, don't worry if you have already engaged in sexual activity. It is possible to change. You can always restart from where you're at. If you commit yourself to not engaging in sexual activity anymore before you are married, your future spouse will probably still appreciate it to a similar degree.

One way to help you preserve yourself for love is by practicing modesty. Modesty is a boundary that is meant to protect you from being used. It can be a controversial one to talk about, but it is important to understand. There is a lot of disagreement about how to practice modesty and many people get this one totally wrong.

Let's start with what modesty means. Modesty is related to the word moderate. Basically, it means being moderate with your behavior. In our modern culture it is often directed towards the way people dress, especially women. The clothing someone wears is important, but it is not the only thing the term modesty can be applied to. It can also include speech or other behaviors. However, since our modern culture puts such an emphasis on clothing, I will begin there.

This can be easy to get wrong. On one extreme, some people think what they wear is irrelevant. If someone wants to show a ton of skin or dress provocatively, people on this side argue that it's an individual's choice to wear whatever they want. It's considered empowering, a casting off of outdated social norms. The problem with this view on modesty is that it underestimates the human propensity for using other people. The reason we wear clothing is to protect us, not only from the elements of nature, but also from objectification by other people. When a person reveals their body, they open themselves up to the eyes of other people using them for pleasure. At the same time, they can be the ones using other people, dressing provocatively to elicit attention. This is easily seen on social media, where many people post sexually suggestive pictures in order to gain likes and followers. In this scenario, both parties are being used. The person revealing their body is being used for their beauty and the viewer is being used for their attention. Notice that neither party is giving or receiving love. Modesty is meant to foster love. That is why it is valuable to practice.

On the other hand, there is another extreme to modesty. This can be seen in cultures where women are required to cover themselves totally, some only being able to reveal their eyes. The problem with this view of modesty is that it can imply that the body is bad. It is restrictive and oppressive, rather than providing the freedom that boundaries are supposed to provide. Another similar error is making modesty about mechanical rules, as often happens in purity culture. Dresses have to be lower than three and a half fingers above the knees and shirts that leave the back part of the shoulders exposed are forbidden. This view of modesty misses the point. It ends up becoming another form of objectification, just with language that makes it sound more righteous.

A proper view of modesty is one that centers around the intentions of one's heart. It is a perspective oriented towards love. Just like any other boundary, it is meant to protect, not restrict. The proper way to practice modesty is to ask yourself whether your behavior is fostering love or not. Is the outfit you wear going to accentuate your beauty or cause people to look at you lustfully? Is your speech stringing someone along seductively or helping people get to know you authentically? If you practice modesty correctly, it should cause people to value you. It will help you accentuate all the good parts about you without giving yourself away too easily. The point isn't to wall yourself off from the world, but to make wise decisions about what you are revealing to people. If you give yourself away too easily, you make yourself vulnerable to being used. Practicing modesty will help you reserve yourself for love.

Another boundary to think about in relationships is the boundary of your time. You might really enjoy being with the person you're dating, and even experience a deep longing to be with them when you're not together, but it's important not to give them all of your time. There are a few reasons for this. Again, the first one is for protection. If you spend all your time with someone and they become the center of your life and then you break up, it can be devastating. It can lead to serious consequences and even cause you to doubt your own worth because your entire life was totally wrapped up in the relationship. Even if you are certain someone is right for you and you plan to get married, it still isn't a good idea to invest every second of your time with them. You should have other things in life that give you purpose and fulfillment. You should have other stable relationships with friends and family. Having good friends outside of the person you are in a romantic relationship with is very important. You need people that are going to be in your corner regardless of the circumstances. You need friends of the same sex to share things with that your spouse simply cannot understand. Having this kind of support will also provide you with freedom as you determine whether someone is right for you. It will give you the ability to walk away from dating someone without the fear of losing everything. You should also think about these boundaries on time in regards to the person you are dating and whether they have them or not.

Do they have things to do outside your relationship? Do they have friends and family members that are important in their life? Do they have a relationship with God and a good prayer life? If they don't, you might find yourself being used in a way you don't desire. If someone is acting overly needy, this could be a red flag, and you will probably feel it as a sense of guilt or discomfort. If the person you are dating wants to spend every waking hour with you, it might be hard for you to find time with your friends, or it might be harder to end the relationship if it isn't working because you fear hurting the other person. There are a lot of things that can go wrong. Having other things going on in your life is important, for both you and your mate. You should have goals and hobbies that are personal to you. Sure, eventually as you get deeper in a relationship with someone, these things might merge to become an important part of both your lives and you will end up spending more and more time together, but you should still maintain appropriate boundaries on time in order to protect the relationship and keep it healthy. Creating space for your mate can also prevent the relationship from getting stagnant, and ensure that you don't fall into boredom.

The next type of boundary that is important for relationships is the emotional boundary. Emotional boundaries are similar to physical boundaries in that they protect us from creating bonds that are likely to cause wounding if broken. Physical intimacy creates emotional bonds, but emotional intimacy also creates emotional bonds. By now you should be getting the point that creating bonds without commitment is risky and can turn very painful if those bonds are broken. Emotional boundaries are a little harder to define, but should still be considered. For example, if you start texting someone "good morning" and "goodnight" every day after your first date, you probably don't have much of an emotional boundary in place, and you might be in dangerous territory. Emotional boundaries might include things like how you speak to someone, how you spend money for them, or how you talk about them with others. Here's another example. If you buy a diamond ring or front row tickets to the World Series for someone you've been on two dates with, how do you think this would affect them emotionally? Would they see this as simply a friendly gesture or would they see this as a major act of commitment? Whenever you are about to do something, think about the message you are sending the other person. A common emotional boundary that is inappropriately crossed is saying "I love you" way too soon. If you are still deciding whether someone is a good match for you, but your actions communicate that you are highly invested in them, it could easily end poorly. In some sense you are actually lying to them! Your intentions and your actions don't line up. Not only are you likely to hurt the other person, but you are likely to hurt yourself. It's best to be honest with others. This doesn't mean confessing your undying love for someone the first time you meet them. That would be an example of not setting good boundaries for yourself, and it will likely scare away everyone you are interested in. What I mean by being honest is that your words and your actions should be congruent. Using this framework we can see how telling someone you love them after one date is a lie. You cannot love someone without consistent commitment or the ability to sacrifice your own desires for the good of the other. If you really loved someone, you would restrain yourself from putting undue pressure on them by confessing your love for them. If you really loved someone, you would let your actions display that love until the level of commitment was made that would allow for confessing it. Again, emotional boundaries allow for clarity in the relationship. I'm not saying that romantic gestures are a bad thing. They just need to be done in the proper context.

Relationships are usually going to do better if they start small and grow over time. When you engage in big romantic gestures early on, you risk burning out quickly. Establishing emotional boundaries will help your relationship grow at the proper pace. When thinking about emotional boundaries, you should also think about your own emotional limits. Maybe the other person is trying to come on too strongly. Maybe they are making you feel uncomfortable. This doesn't necessarily mean you should end the relationship, but it might be a red flag. The other person might not have had good teaching on relationships or maybe they come from a broken home. What you should do is establish boundaries and tell them very clearly what is appropriate and what is not. If you set a boundary and the other person keeps crossing it repeatedly, then you have to enforce some consequences. If they still don't respect your limits, it might be time to eject. However, if they are doing their best to stop the problematic behavior, then you could continue the relationship if you thought it was worth it. It might even make your relationship stronger because you will have resolved a conflict together. None of us are perfect, and you will never find anyone if you expect perfection right off the bat. Be firm in your boundaries, but forgiving when people fail to meet your expectations.

The final boundary I want to cover here is one that is often overlooked. That is the spiritual boundary. The realm of the spirit is not a tangible material thing that you experience with your senses. That doesn't mean that it is any less important to maintain boundaries here. Your spiritual life can be one of the most intimate parts of your existence. Not everyone needs to know what is happening between you and God. Not everyone needs to know how much time you spend in prayer or what good deeds you've done. Let me be clear. I'm not saying you shouldn't talk about God, or never share anything that is happening spiritually. There is a time and place for it. Let me give you an example to illustrate what I mean. Imagine you are friends with someone who is married. Your friend might tell you some things about his marriage, but you wouldn't expect him to tell you his wife's most intimate secrets. There are things married couples share communally, and there are things that they only share between themselves. It's the same with God. "But when you pray, go into your room and shut the door and pray to your Father who is in secret. And your Father who sees in secret will reward you." (Matthew 6:6)

One time I went on a first date with this girl. It was very casual at first. We just went to a park and talked. However, after the park, I invited the girl to go to a church with me and pray together. I thought, "Couples should pray together so that God will direct them in their relationship. We might as well start now if this is going to turn into anything." The problem was that we weren't a couple. It was a first date. Nothing horrible happened, but it felt awkward and inappropriate. The girl called me a couple days later and said she just wanted to be friends. I never asked this girl if praying together was part of the reason she friend zoned me, but I suspect it at least played a part. Like I said already, your spiritual life can be an extremely intimate part of your life. When I brought this girl into my spiritual life right off the bat, it probably overwhelmed her. It probably felt similar to the example I gave earlier of buying a diamond ring or front row tickets to a world series baseball game, but even more so because of the intimate personal nature of our spiritual lives. That's why it is important to set boundaries in this area. It could mean choosing to pray on your own until you are in a committed relationship. It could mean getting a pastor or other mentor to share spiritual matters with, instead of relying on your mate. Like all boundaries, this doesn't mean they can't change over time or that you will never be able to pray with your significant other. It's simply about being wise about what you share so that you are protected from dangerous situations. Imagine if you began dating someone and you started praying with them regularly. What happens when they break up with you? Not only would it be painful, but it could jeopardize your relationship with God. You may get angry at Him because the other person hurt you. Yet, God is precisely the one you want to fall back on in a situation like that. Therefore, it's a good idea to set some boundaries so you don't wind up in that situation in the first place.

I hope you can see the value in setting boundaries a little better now. Boundaries are there for protection, but they can also strengthen relationships. If you don't have much experience with them, they can certainly seem daunting. I won't lie. Even if you do understand them, it can be hard to actually implement them, especially if you haven't had good ones in the past. It will take some practice and you are going to fail from time to time. Don't be too hard on yourself. Start with small boundaries if you need to. For now, it is simply important that you know they exist, that they are there for your protection, and you understand that they will strengthen your relationships if you implement them well. As long as you start making progress, you are on the right track.

CHAPTER 6

VIRTUE

Now we are going to look at another aspect of good relationships that will help you to put into practice everything I have been talking about. This aspect is virtue. Virtue is defined as moral excellence and righteousness. It is the ability to choose to do the right thing quickly and with ease. Some examples of virtues are prudence, temperance, courage, and chastity. Prudence, for instance, is careful, good judgment that allows someone to avoid danger or risks. It is good thinking and decision making. Chastity is all about valuing one's body and sexuality. The virtues also have opposites, which are called vices. Some examples of vices are foolishness, gluttony, cowardice, and lust. Vices are evil and immoral habits. They make it easy to choose the bad and difficult to do what is right. You might be wondering what this all has to do with relationships. Well, if virtue is the ability to act rightly and do what is good, then it is actually required in order to have good relationships. So far we've said multiple times that loving someone involves doing what is best for them. If you don't have virtue, you don't even have the ability to do what is good, and if you don't have the ability to do what is good, then you can't love someone because love involves doing what is good. Vice will take this problem even further because you will not only lack the ability to love, but you will actually do harm to others.

The virtues are also very practical. They involve concrete steps you can start taking right now. They can be practiced and you can grow in them. For example, if you want to grow in temperance, which is moderation and self-restraint, you could deny yourself from having dessert more than once per day or limit your time on the internet to a certain amount. Understanding virtue is also important because when you get into a serious relationship, your virtues and your vices are greatly magnified. If you are angry and unkind on your own, this is only going to be exacerbated once you are in a relationship. However, if you are courageous or prudent, those qualities will also be enhanced and being in a relationship will allow you to become an even better person.

One virtue that is clearly tied to relationships is the virtue of chastity. Chastity is the ability to refrain from engaging in physical intimacy outside of the proper context. It's all about valuing one's body and sexuality, which means it is strongly related to what we have already been talking about! I do want to clarify something here that is commonly misunderstood.

Chastity is not the same as celibacy. It doesn't mean that you never engage in sex for the entirety of your life. It means you save it for marriage and never engage in it strictly for personal pleasure at the expense of the other person. Chastity means never using someone else as an object or strictly for your own pleasure. Remember, you are a unique, unrepeatable person with dignity and value. Chastity is about choosing what will uphold and protect that dignity and value, for both you and your mate. Actually, all the virtues will help you accomplish this to some degree.

A bonus to the virtues is that they are also very attractive. It isn't easy to be a virtuous person. Doing the right thing isn't always doing the most pleasurable thing. In fact, most of the time it's not doing the pleasurable thing. It often means doing extremely difficult things. For that reason, virtue is also attractive, at least to the type of people you want in your life. Living virtuously will likely repel vicious people who will hurt and use you, unless they themselves are trying to change.

It is becoming more and more rare to meet people who are virtuous. If you begin to grow in virtue, you will stand out from other people. Again, some people aren't going to like it, but the right people will. You will attract people who are also virtuous and these are people who are going to make your life better. They will choose to do what is good rather than simply what feels best or is easiest. They will sacrifice their own desires for your good. This actually brings me to another important part of dating involving virtue.

I already talked a little bit about what you should look for in a mate, but this one is key. Something you should be trying to determine as you date someone is if they possess virtue. Why is it so important? Well, think about it. Do you want someone who is going to cheat on you? No. Well, the virtuous person is going to be the one who doesn't cheat because they have a habit of being honest and value chastity. Do you want someone who blows all your money on shopping? No. Again, the virtuous person is going to be the one that doesn't do that because they are temperate. The virtuous person is going to be authentic and genuine. You can better rely on them to do what is good and this will make life much better for you, rather than worse. This is yet another reason relationships should be given time to grow. The only way to determine if someone is virtuous is by seeing how they act in different situations. They might be kind and loving when things are going well, but how do they act when they encounter hardship or disaster? You have to spend enough time with someone to witness how they act in different circumstances. A desire for finding a virtuous mate is also another reason for not engaging in physical intimacy right away. If someone is able to sacrifice their desire for physical pleasure, they are more likely to be a virtuous person. It is a sign in itself that the person will be a good one to build a relationship with. Learning about and growing in virtue can be difficult, but it is absolutely worth the difficulty.

So, how does one grow in virtue? Here are a couple tips. First, learn what the virtues are. Some of the major ones are prudence, temperance, fortitude, justice, faith, hope, and love. I can give a brief description of each one to get you started.

As I already mentioned, prudence is careful, good judgment that allows someone to avoid danger or unnecessary risks. Temperance is the ability to control one's appetite. This isn't only in regards to one's appetite for food, but any earthly thing a person might desire. It is the ability to deny yourself anything that goes beyond what is needed. Fortitude is courage in pain or adversity. It is the ability to endure difficult things without giving up. Justice is giving people what they are due. It means not cheating or robbing from others. It means repairing things when they have been broken, including relationships. Faith is a spiritual virtue that means to put all of your trust in God and His plan for things. It means trusting even when something doesn't make sense. Hope is believing that there is good in the future. It is related to faith in that it involves trust. When someone has hope, they trust that even the negative circumstances they go through will ultimately lead to good. Finally, love is doing what is good for others, and helping them to do what is good themselves. It is freely giving of oneself in order that others will benefit from it.

I know that was only a very brief summary of those virtues, and that isn't even all of them! But hopefully this will give you an idea of what they are all about. There is overlap between them all and this is mostly about developing good character as a whole anyways. If you want to go more in depth, there are many resources out there that can help you do that.

My next tip is to pick just one of the virtues and focus on improving that one thing. Be aware of all of them, and try your best to live them out, but focus your effort on just one. This will help you to not get overwhelmed. Once you pick one, start making small decisions that will help you grow in that virtue. Since virtue is the ability to do the right thing, the simplest way to grow in virtue is to determine what is right, true, and good and try to live your life in accord with that. A great place to start is the Bible. The Bible is where the moral foundations for all of western society were gathered from, and it contains the true moral foundation for all of humanity. It provides a clear outline for what is right, true, and good. It can help you understand this in a way that is far beyond the scope of this book. I'm just here to get you started on the right track with the knowledge that virtue exists and that growing in virtue will help your relationships become more successful. It is actually required in order to have good relationships because love is choosing to do what is good for other people, and you can only do that if you have virtue.

CHAPTER 7

GOOD RELATIONSHIPS
SUMMARY

We've covered quite a bit of material, so let's take a minute to reflect on where we've been so far. First, I want to emphasize that you are a unique, unrepeatable person with dignity and value. I'm going to continue hammering that idea in throughout this book because knowing your identity is the most important foundation there is for having successful relationships. You need to know that you are valuable and that other people are valuable too. This will determine whether you treat someone as a gift or as an object for use. It will determine whether you feel confident when interacting with someone or anxious and unsure. You need to know who you are because you can't move forward if you don't. We've also established that love is a free gift of yourself that is motivated by desiring the good of others. Love is not simply an emotional feeling. It involves feelings, but it also involves choosing what will actually be most beneficial for someone.

After this we dove into what a good romantic relationship looks like. A good romantic relationship is between one man and one woman, and it has a clear purpose. Dating is not just a recreational activity. The point of dating is to determine whether another person is good for marriage or not. In order to do this well you need to set boundaries. Boundaries are there for your protection. They help you stay detached from deceitful desires as you determine whether someone will make a good mate or not. They prevent you from creating and breaking emotional bonds, which can cause major wounds if done recklessly. Boundaries help you evaluate your relationship with clarity.

Finally, we talked about virtue and how it is necessary for a good relationship. If love is choosing to do what is good for someone, you need to actually have the capability of doing that, which is what virtue is. Pursuing virtue is well worth the effort because not only will it help you have better relationships, it will improve your life overall, and allow you to be joyful and content. Next we are going to dive into complementarity, which is how masculine and feminine energy work together.

CHAPTER 8

COMPLEMENTARITY

Men and women are different. Yes, I said it. Many people in today's world don't want to admit it, but it's true. The sooner we can acknowledge this truth, the sooaner we can move forward and figure out how to best live out our lives as men and women. This doesn't mean that men can't have feminine qualities and women can't have masculine ones. We all exist on a spectrum and have differing levels of masculine and feminine traits. Some men are very feminine and some women are very masculine. However, the average man is going to be more masculine than the average woman and the average woman is going to be more feminine than the average man. When I talk about masculinity, I'm referring to traits that are generally considered more masculine such as assertiveness, analytical thinking, and risk taking. When I talk about femininity, I'm referring to traits that are generally considered more feminine such as being nurturing, capacity for emotional connection, and receptivity. Again, this doesn't mean that only men can be assertive or analytical, or that only women can connect on an emotional level or be receptive. I'm simply pointing out that the traits men generally exhibit are the masculine ones, and the traits women generally exhibit are the feminine ones.

Men and women also differ physically. Men have higher bone density, broader shoulders, and greater muscle mass. Women have wider hips, softer features, and are generally smaller. There are also obvious differences in sex organs, which in themselves provide a certain display of the assertiveness of men and receptivity of women. The male sex organs are outward and penetrating. The testicles produce an endless army of sperm. The female sex organs are inward and receptive. All the eggs a woman will ever have are there from the beginning. The womb is a nurturing environment for offspring to develop. Genetically, men have XY chromosomes and women have XX chromosomes. All of these things show that men and women are different, and that's totally fine. There isn't any reason we need to be exactly the same. The differences between men and women are beautiful and should be viewed as gifts. Just because men are physically stronger doesn't mean they are better than women, and just because women are stronger communicators doesn't mean they are better than men. Men and women are meant to complement each other. When we embrace these God given sexual differences, we improve each other's lives.

Look at the rest of the natural world. It is full of a diversity of species all working together in different ways. If you remove even the smallest species from an ecosystem, it can destroy the entire thing. I remember hearing about this piece of land in Yellowstone National Park that had become desolate. It was once filled with vegetation and streams of water, but it had become dry and desert-like. Someone hypothesized that there were too many deer that were eating all the plants, so they reintroduced wolves into the ecosystem. Quickly, the wolves began hunting the deer, and the vegetation had a chance to grow back. Once that happened, water started collecting and eventually the entire place became a luscious forest again.[8] When we try to remove sex differences between men and women, we end up destroying each other. There is a delicate balance that needs to occur for life to flourish.

Besides, without complementarity life would be boring. Complementarity forces us to get outside ourselves. It shows us that we aren't meant to live life on our own. "It is not good that man should be alone." (Genesis 2:18) We were literally created in such a way that we are missing necessary traits that are held by the opposite sex. This shows us that we need others. When we embrace our weaknesses it allows us to see others' strengths and vice versa. It allows us to help others and let them help us. As men and women, it can literally lead to the creation of new life through procreation. So how do we embrace this complementarity and live in a way that utilizes it to make our lives better?

First, we have to understand the differences between men and women. If you don't acknowledge something even exists, it is hard to use it. The differences between men and women might seem like they should be obvious, but modern culture has done a great job of confusing people on this subject. Right now, it is politically incorrect to say that there are any differences between men and women at all. If someone says that men are physically stronger than women, someone else will point to an example of an extremely strong woman and try to claim that women are just as strong because there is this one example of a strong woman. But like I stated earlier, masculine and feminine traits exist on a spectrum with the average male being more masculine and the average female being more feminine. The strongest male in the world is always going to be stronger than the strongest female in the world, and the average male is always going to be stronger than the average female. This isn't pseudo science. This isn't simply a social construct. These are biological and psychological truths, grounded in facts, that have been observed consistently and persistently throughout all human populations for all of human history. The fact that men and women are different has only been questioned recently due to cultural pressures, and this has come with devastating consequences such as people being confused about their own identity. This is likely a contributor to a lot of the increases in life dissatisfaction and the breakdown of the family we've seen as well. When we try to force people into being something they are not meant to be, there are going to be consequences. You can't use a hammer to drill in a screw. That's why it is so important that we understand the differences between men and women, and who we were created to be. This might seem restrictive on the surface, but it is actually incredibly freeing. It is a lot more fun to do something when you know how to do it correctly. If this applies to games and hobbies, how much more so the fundamental aspects of life that make us human! If you don't know the basic rules for playing basketball, for example, you aren't going to be able to play the game, you probably won't have any fun, and you certainly aren't going to master it. The same goes for life. If you don't understand what kind of traits men usually have and you are a man, you aren't going to be able to play the game of life correctly and you certainly aren't going to be able to master it. The same goes for women. I've already mentioned some of the traits men and women have, but now I'll try to go a little deeper.

CHAPTER 9

MASCULINITY

Since I'm a man, let's start with masculinity. What makes a man masculine? There are many traits that are considered masculine. Each man will have varying levels of these traits. Having more of one or another doesn't make you better or worse than anyone else from a value standpoint, though having these traits may make you better or worse at specific activities. What I'm saying is that evaluating these traits isn't meant to be a judge of character, though embracing masculine traits as a man can be a tool to help develop good character. You can be a man who is not super aggressive or analytical and still be a good man and person. You are still valuable in the eyes of God. It might simply mean that your purpose isn't to become a fighter pilot. Maybe you are more suited to becoming an artist. A lot of this stuff isn't in our control. Many of these traits are determined by our genetic makeup. We have to make the best of what we've been given. However, it is possible to harness the genetic predisposition you have towards any given masculine trait in order to best utilize it in a virtuous way. For example, if you are genetically predisposed to being hyper aggressive, you can work on this trait in order to direct it towards something good like becoming a police officer rather than becoming a thief who beats up innocent people and robs them.

If you are a man it is good to develop these masculine traits, though it will take an incredible amount of intentional hard work, especially if you are not naturally predisposed to the trait you want to work on. For example, if you want to become more assertive and this trait isn't part of your natural personality, you will have to practice being assertive intensely and persistently, and it will likely be difficult even then. I'm not saying you can't do it or shouldn't do it, but you should really think about whether you want a given trait or not. If there is a specific goal you have that requires utilizing that trait, then it might be worth it to try and grow in it. Otherwise you might just want to focus on playing to your strengths. There is plenty of opportunity to grow regardless of where you put the emphasis. Even your weaknesses can become strengths if looked at from the right perspective. What I mean by that is that when it comes to relationships, people don't actually want to be with people who are perfect, though it might seem like that at times. Being vulnerable about your weaknesses can actually serve to make people like you more. Again, that shouldn't be the goal of revealing your weaknesses. You shouldn't just go around vomiting all of your problems on people. It's more like an openness and willingness to share our weaknesses instead of trying to hide them. In a weird paradox, this actually shows us to be stronger.

We should also be unwilling to pretend we have skills or abilities that we don't actually have. This is about being authentic. Think of the characters from great stories that are the most likable. Why are they likable? It's often because they have some flaw that we can relate to. Maybe it's that they are afraid of something and have to overcome that fear to reach their goals, or maybe it's that they grew up in poverty before becoming successful. Whatever the case, these are usually the characters we connect with the most in stories. Notice how I didn't only mention the weaknesses a character might have had, but that they were able to embrace those weaknesses or overcome them. Looking at our weaknesses as strengths doesn't mean we give up and say, "Poor me. I'm so weak. I'll never do anything good." No! It means being willing to acknowledge our weaknesses and then go after our goals despite them. This takes incredible courage, and courage is a masculine trait. Courage isn't fearlessness. It's experiencing fear, but taking action anyways.

There are two types of courage, physical and moral. Physical courage is taking action though there is risk of physical pain or injury. Moral courage is choosing to do what is right even though it might lead to negative social, economic, or other consequences. Other words synonymous with courage are bravery and fortitude. Think of men going into battle, or leading social revolutions. They often need great courage to accomplish these things. Courage doesn't always mean entering into over the top life threatening situations though. When it comes to relationships, courage could be as simple as walking up to a stranger to say hello, or asking a girl out on a date. There is a risk of rejection in those situations, but you are willing to take action despite that risk. This is both masculine and attractive to women. Courage demonstrates that you are less likely to wimp out in the face of a challenge that threatens your family. It demonstrates that you aren't going to change because of social pressure or other external factors. Therefore, it demonstrates that you would make a good mate. Courage demonstrates a willingness to protect what matters. Most women are probably not consciously thinking about these things when they are with men, but they are powerful biological drivers that will make them feel attracted to them. This is the case with a lot of the masculine traits.

Take analytical thinking for example. You might think that this would not be very helpful when it comes to attracting women, who are much more emotionally driven. But what does analytical thinking help you do? It allows you to solve problems, and many women want a man who can solve problems for them. Though, I need to clarify something here. Most women also want a man who can listen, and sometimes they will get upset if you try to solve their problems. Sometimes they just want to feel heard. This can be tricky for men to figure out. Sometimes you have to go beyond the direct meaning of the words a woman uses. Women communicate on multiple different levels at the same time. This is why hearing the words, "I'm fine," means you better believe you're in big trouble. Still, problem solving can be a very desirable trait. If you're a man, pay attention the next time you're with a woman. Try to notice if she brings up anything that might be a problem she wants solved. You will have to pay attention because, again, she isn't always going to state the problem directly. She will more likely allude to it. For example, if her door handle is broken, she probably won't say, "My door handle is broken. Can you fix it?" More likely she will say something like, "This stupid door handle never works right!" That's your cue to step in and offer help. If you are a man who is an analytical thinker, it might make it harder to connect with some women, but it will also be very attractive to many of them. Masculine traits are attractive to women on a very primal level, just as feminine traits are attractive to men on that same level. It won't always make sense, but this is how we are wired. It's about complementarity. Again, the masculine and feminine aren't supposed to be the same thing. They are meant to complement each other.

The final masculine quality I will go over is leadership. Masculine men take charge and lead others. This might be in the context of business or sports, or it might simply mean guiding their families. If a man is a leader in one area, he will likely be a leader in other areas as well. There are many aspects to leadership. It doesn't mean you just boss people around. That would actually be an example of poor leadership. True leaders serve the people they lead. They enter into situations alongside them. They teach. They assist. They sacrifice. Leadership is not easy, but it is a masculine trait that is worth developing if you are a man.

Though women can lead, leadership is generally a more masculine trait, and women are often attracted to men who lead. The feminine is more inclined to follow and support. Men who take charge and lead generally complement those qualities well, therefore becoming very attractive to feminine women. In the context of relationships, the man, as spiritual head, is to lay the groundwork and establish the direction of the relationship. This doesn't mean a man should dominate the relationship, or make every single decision. Remember that leadership is about service. It simply means that the man should generally set the tone for and guide the relationship. He should provide safety and security. This becomes even more critical with marriage and family. The man needs to make sure his family is cared for and protected. He needs to set the rules for his household. If the man doesn't lead, his household will likely fall into chaos and disorder. His children won't respect him and his wife will resent him. The masculine man takes charge and leads his family. He leads in all the areas of life where he is competent. He shares his knowledge with others. He is loving, generous, and genuinely lifts others up with him. The masculine man is a dangerous man who is in control of himself. He has the ability to inflict incredible damage, but only uses it when absolutely necessary, such as in the protection of others who are weaker than him. The masculine is both powerful and gentle. It is not a macho emotionless display of brute force, and it is not a weak passive placating that panders to the blowing of the wind. It is a tender strength under control. Now that we've looked at the masculine, let's switch gears to the feminine.

CHAPTER 10

FEMININITY

It's difficult to describe the feminine in the same way I described the masculine, simply because it is a totally different kind of energy. The masculine is very straightforward and ordered, whereas the feminine is more emotional and spontaneous. Again, one isn't better than the other. It is simply more difficult to describe the feminine in a straightforward analytical way. Something like poetry or song would probably be better suited to the task. However, that's not the style of this book or the way I think, so I will do my best to describe the feminine using the same style I've been using so far. This whole section is only a brief discussion on complementarity anyways. It is only meant to show that it exists and give a basic idea of what it is. There is plenty of room to go much deeper into the subject that simply isn't possible within the scope of this book.

Some of the traits that are considered feminine are receptivity, emotional connection, and being nurturing. Women are naturally more suited to empathize with others because they can easily connect on an emotional level. The feminine feels emotions very deeply. This is sometimes described as intuition. Women who are very feminine have an uncanny ability to sense another's internal state. This can be extremely valuable. For example, through this intuition women can tell if someone is hurting, or if they are untrustworthy. It is one of the reasons women are so good with children. They can sense what a child is feeling and what that child needs. This emotional sensitivity can motivate them to charity and caring for others. It's why you will find more women in the nursing profession than you will find as doctors. Doctors are usually very analytical. They have to diagnose diseases and solve problems. They are often more detached from the patient. Nurses are the ones who are in there caring for the patient day in and day out. This doesn't mean women can't be doctors and men can't be nurses. I'm simply using these professions as a way to highlight the masculine and feminine.

The feminine is also very receptive. This can translate into hospitality, for example. Many women love to host and entertain people. They like to make others feel at home. This is a manifestation of the womb, which is a biological part of a woman's hospitality.

The feminine is also associated with beauty. Men tend to be more rugged, physically and mentally. Women tend to have a softness and smoothness to them that gives them a certain beauty. You may often hear people compliment women by saying things like, "She was glowing!" This is interesting because men tend to be more visually stimulated in their attractions, whereas women are often more mentally stimulated in their attractions. One way for women to attract men is to highlight their physical beauty in some way. Men usually are not attracted to rugged or rough looking women, though women are often attracted to these things in men. It's because the masculine is attracted to the feminine and the feminine is not rough or rugged. The feminine is inviting and receptive.

Women who emphasize their feminine traits are going to be more attractive to the masculine. Again, this doesn't mean that women can't be strong or analytical. I am talking in broad generalizations to help you understand this dance between the masculine and feminine. The more masculine a man is, the more he is going to desire a very feminine woman and vice versa. A more feminine man might pair well with a more masculine woman. The point is that masculine and feminine complement each other.

As for relationships, a feminine woman is often more likely to follow the lead of the man. She is going to be more supportive in her role, though I have to firmly emphasize that this doesn't mean she has a secondary role. I'm simply stating that the way the feminine complements the masculine is by following and supporting. It doesn't mean a woman can't have her own goals or desires. It doesn't mean a woman can't make decisions. It just means that with respect to the relationship, the feminine is more apt to follow the lead of the masculine. If men and women can get over their egos and accept this, it can be incredibly powerful. Men shouldn't try to dominate women and women shouldn't try to usurp leadership. Rather, working together in a complementary way, they should help each other in the specific ways they were designed to. This will allow for more freedom and more happiness.

CHAPTER 11

LOVE AND RESPECT

So how do masculine and feminine complement each other? How do men and women work together? A major part of it is love and respect. The feminine desires love and the masculine desires respect. This is something that is often misunderstood, especially in today's culture. For example, women are often told two major lies. The first is that men only want them for sex. This often leads to promiscuity, manipulative behavior, and self-objectification. It degrades women and can cause them to devalue themselves, while simultaneously losing the respect of men. On the other side of the coin is the lie that women who accomplish success in their careers or make a lot of money will have something other than sex to bring to the table. Unfortunately, this also often leads to similar problems. Most men don't really care if a woman is successful or has a lot of money. It may make her slightly more attractive to some men, but the amount of attraction that is added is almost irrelevant because of what masculinity desires. What most men really desire is loyalty and respect. If a woman brings those things to a relationship, a man will treasure her more than the most precious of jewels.

There are also some lies men are told. The first is that all women really desire jerks. There is a certain amount of truth to that, but it is distorted. Most women desire men who are strong and protective. Due to their disagreeable nature, jerks often have those traits. However, they are severely lacking in love, which is what the feminine truly desires. Jerks can seem great in the short term, but they usually don't do well in the long run. They lack empathy. They lack the ability to listen. They lack the ability to compromise. Jerks are men that will usually leave women heartbroken.

The other side of this coin is the proverbial nice guy. The nice guy believes that he should pour everything he has into the woman he wants. He brings her gifts. He talks to her about her problems. He does everything he can to please her. The problem with the nice guy is that he lacks strength and lets people walk all over him. He is unable to lead. He is unable to protect the woman. The nice guy doesn't spark any strong feelings in women, so he ends up perpetually in the friend zone. The feminine desires to be both led and loved. The jerk can lead, but can't love. The nice guy can love, but can't lead. A truly masculine man will be able to do both. This will gain him the respect of women, and he will respond with love. A complementary relationship happens when women are loved and men are respected. In these types of relationships, both the masculine and feminine desires are being fulfilled.

CHAPTER 5

COMPLEMENTARITY CONCLUSION

To summarize, there is both masculine and feminine energy. These energies can be a powerful force for motivation, relationships, and creativity. Think of all the men who solved societal problems out of their masculine energy, or all the women who cared for others in heroic ways using their feminine energy. When we embrace our God given masculinity or femininity, we can channel that energy into doing great things. When both masculine and feminine energy come together, it is even more powerful. The greatest example of this is when a man and a woman come together and create a new human life through procreation.

Complementarity is all about getting masculine and feminine energy working together. There is a certain polarity between them, which actually strengthens the bond between men and women in the same way the positive and negative fields draw magnets together. Masculine energy is very outward and feminine energy is very receptive. If these can work together it creates a magnetic energy that can be used for all sorts of endeavors. Instead of looking at masculinity and femininity as opposites that are in conflict with each other, if we look at them as complementary energies that are strongest when working together, it allows for great power. When we see them as opposites we tend to feel resentment and anger towards those who have energy that is different than our own. If we can learn to see masculine and feminine as complementary, we become more collaborative and express greater unity. We should embrace our masculine and feminine differences because they will help us strengthen our bonds with each other and accomplish great things.

CHAPTER 13

INTRO TO INNER CONFIDENCE

Some often repeated dating advice is "just be yourself." This is true in a sense, but if you don't know who you actually are or you aren't currently living up to your potential, "just be yourself" becomes a useless platitude. Being yourself only works when you actually know your identity and have developed yourself enough to value who you are. It only works when you are living up to your God-given potential, not squandering life, but rather giving it your best shot. This doesn't mean you have to look like a supermodel, be as funny as Dave Chapelle, or have the riches of Elon Musk. It simply means that you have to be comfortable with the person God made you to be, that you have developed some virtue or are working towards it, and that you have your life together enough that you actually have something to offer other people. If you are unsure of your identity, are an angry, greedy person, and all you do is play video games all day, you probably aren't going to attract anyone and even if you could, you probably shouldn't. Love is about doing what's good for other people, and if you don't have your own life together, or aren't at least working to improve it, you won't be able to do what is good for other people. You can't give what you don't have. So how do you figure out your identity and develop the type of confidence that will make you attractive? That's what I'm going to write about next.

Who Are You?

You might be getting sick of me saying this, but I'm going to say it again. You are a unique, unrepeatable person with dignity and value. I keep repeating it because it's the number one most important thing you need to understand. I'm not just telling this to you because I think it will make you feel good. I actually mean it. Every person that exists is made in the image and likeness of God. Whether they live in a way that reflects that or not is going to vary, but regardless, it is still the truth. You have inherent and inexpressible value that cannot be taken away from you. No matter what you've done, no matter who you think you are, your value as a human exists. It isn't dependent on your finances. It isn't dependent on your looks. It isn't dependent on how many friends you have. In God's eyes you are a treasure. You are valuable and worthy of love. You have a unique gift that no one else possesses. This doesn't mean that everyone else is going to see that gift in you, or that you will even see it in yourself, but nevertheless it is there. It's up to you whether you share it or not.

In order to do that, you have to realize the gift is there and then treat yourself in a manner worthy of that gift. Again, this is one of the reasons why it is so important for you to understand this truth. If you don't believe you have value, you won't act like you have value, and no one will respect you, including yourself. In fact, it will likely serve to further decrease your view of yourself and create a vicious cycle where you think poorly of yourself, which causes others to treat you poorly, which in turn causes you to think even more poorly of yourself. If you want to become more attractive, that is not what you want. People are attracted to things that have value. When someone is confident about themselves, others tend to believe they have more value. This can create the opposite of the negative feedback loop I just mentioned. In this virtuous cycle, you view yourself as someone valuable, which causes others to treat you respectfully, which causes you to gain even more confidence.

Now I realize that just telling you that you are valuable probably isn't going to make you believe it, but I'm going to do my best to help get you to that point. Part of the reason I keep reminding you of your value is because repeating it will hopefully bring this truth to mind more often. This is especially important because society is constantly barraging you with voices that tell you that you are worthless, or that you are only valuable for your body, money, intelligence, or whatever other trait they want to emphasize to sell something. Marketers understand the power of planting ideas in your mind. The more you hear something, the more likely you are to believe it. So like it or not, I'm going to keep reminding you that you are a unique, unrepeatable person with dignity and value.

Unfortunately, just hearing that a bunch of times isn't the only thing that needs to happen for you to become truly confident. Even if I told you that you're valuable 77,000 times throughout this book, it wouldn't get you where you need to be to become attractive and successful in relationships. I wish it were that easy, but anything worthwhile takes effort. There is a lot more you are going to have to do to build the kind of confidence that will be unshakeable, but I will do my best to help you get there because I know it is well worth it.

CHAPTER 14

EMOTIONAL HEALING
AND
LETTING GO

One of the first things you should get started on is emotional healing and dealing with past traumas. Today I was talking with a woman when her young daughter ran up. The girl had a very sour expression on her face. I asked her what was going on. "I have to go to a new school and I don't like it!" Her mom said something along the lines of, "Don't be upset about it. Just be happy." I forget the exact wording, but that was the gist of it, which should serve to illustrate my point.

The world tries to tell us that our emotions are bad. From the day we are born, we are conditioned to think happiness is the only emotion that is good or acceptable. The world says, "If you aren't happy there is something wrong with you." This works out great for marketers. Not happy? It's because you don't have the thing they are trying to sell you. It's because you don't have the best car or because you aren't beautiful enough or any number of things, and the solution just happens to be the very thing they are trying to sell. We often end up buying that thing, we feel a quick burst of satisfaction, and then before we know it we go back to the same state we were in before. We still aren't happy, so we think it must be because something else is missing. We might even blame ourselves for this imagined problem. "I'm not happy, so there must be something wrong with me." How many people believe they are mentally ill simply because they feel anger or sadness and the world shames them for it? What if we did what the Bible says?

"Rejoice with those who rejoice, weep with those who weep." (Romans 12:15)

Imagine that feeling all the emotions was welcomed and acceptable. How would that change your perspective? Would it not make you value the full range of emotions? Now let me be clear, this doesn't mean we should give free reign to all of our emotions. That can be dangerous too. Feeling anger doesn't mean it's good to go smash in your ex boyfriend's windshield just because you felt like it. What I'm talking about is simply recognizing that emotions other than happiness are part of the human experience, and having them doesn't mean you are broken. These emotions are not something to beat yourself up over or to stuff down inside. We need to be able to feel them completely and process them so they don't cause long term negative effects.

That is often why our past traumas cause problems later in life. We experienced something that made us feel an emotion, but instead of processing that emotion, we learned some other type of coping mechanism that has stuck with us, even though it no longer serves us and causes dysfunction in our lives. For example, imagine the girl from my earlier story felt shamed for being told not to be sad about having to change schools. Imagine that when she grows up, she puts on a fake smile when she is actually angry or sad about something. Even though the mom's reaction to the girl's comment might seem like a small thing, it could end up leading to severe dysfunction in her life. She may begin to resent people who make her mad or struggle with communication issues. She may build up so many walls that she feels isolated and alone and that nobody understands her. She may try to find her worth in material items or beauty. Maybe she even develops multiple personality disorder or some other severe psychological illness. That is probably unlikely to occur from one small comment, but if she is repeatedly told that it is not ok to feel anything but happiness throughout her childhood, you can see how it might lead to these kinds of outcomes. That's why it's important to understand how this happens and recognize where it might be happening in our own lives.

How much pressure would it take off of you if you knew that you didn't always have to be happy? Would that relief in itself not actually make you happier? There is a great irony to all this. When you allow yourself to feel these so-called "negative" emotions, it actually allows you to feel the "positive" ones more fully too. Years of suppressing anger, sadness, and loneliness conditions us to not only suppress those emotions, but also joy, peace, hope, and all the other emotions as well. As we allow ourselves to feel the painful emotions again, we are able to start feeling our positive emotions more strongly too.

For example, many people aren't able to laugh. I realize that might sound crazy, but it's truly a problem for a lot of people. They seriously can't laugh. Think about your own life. When was the last time you laughed out loud? I mean really laughed out loud. Not just a chuckle. I'm talking about a guttural laugh that is completely unstifled. Are you able to do it? Again, this isn't a problem for everyone, but many people aren't able to laugh like this and some can't laugh at all. It's not because they don't want to. They have simply stifled their emotions for so long that they have erected a giant barrier to expressing what they feel.

I know because I was one of those people for a long time. I struggled showing or feeling any emotion at all. I was so afraid of revealing anything about myself that when I would go to the bathroom, I developed this anxiety around peeing. I couldn't pee if there were other people around. I would actually pretend I had to poop so I could use the stall with a door on it. That was the only way I could pee, even if I had to go extremely bad. I suppressed everything. I was living in a state of fear and apathy. It was so bad that I vividly remember the first time I actually felt emotion after years of being stifled. It was right after I encountered Jesus in a dream. There was this powerful moment when He forgave me despite all the horrible things I had done. It was so powerful that I started weeping. I had hardly shed a tear for years and years, even after breaking my back and becoming paralyzed, and yet here I was sobbing. Afterwards I felt amazing. It was like the floodgates had broken and I was suddenly free. That wasn't the end of it. There was also some deeper healing that needed to happen over time, but it was a huge first step in the process. I was alone when this originally occurred, and it took a while for me to get to the point where I was able to show emotion around other people again. Still, there was a clear distinction between the emotionally suppressed state I had been living in and the strong feelings I began experiencing.

Another important point to note is that this is an ongoing process. The more we allow ourselves to feel and display the authentic emotions that arise within us, the freer we become. On top of that, by revealing those emotions to others, it allows us to connect with them on a much deeper level. All of us are human, despite what the world wants us to believe. We have ups and downs. We have times of great pleasure and times of great suffering. These things are universal to all of us. Being vulnerable with our emotions allows other people to feel understood. "Hey this person deals with the same stuff I deal with." That makes emotional healing a necessary step on the way to having better relationships. It's not easy. It's going to take a lot of work. You might even have to get professional help. It will probably require bringing up painful experiences from years ago that you have never dealt with. In fact, it can even be a good thing to ask yourself questions that will bring up those painful memories. Why do I believe I'm not good enough? Why do I believe I am unlovable? Etc. Use a journal to write down whatever comes up. Try to get to the root causes of your behaviors. Like I said, it might take some help from a friend or therapist. There are many different methods to going about it. The point is that you do something. The freedom and all the other benefits you will experience are absolutely worth it.

CHAPTER 15

ATTACHMENT THEORY

There is an idea about relationships in the field of psychology called attachment theory. Basically, this is the idea that the relational attachments a person forms during their early childhood greatly impact their social and emotional development and will predict the quality and types of relationships they form later in life.[9] This is similar to what I was describing with the little girl being upset about changing schools in the previous chapter, but let me give you another example that is more descriptive.

Imagine a child gets angry about something. He doesn't do anything harmful or destructive. He simply expresses the emotion of anger. Perhaps he can't figure out how a toy works. The child's mother doesn't consider his emotional state acceptable so she punishes him by locking him in his room and leaving him alone. Imagine the child's confusion at this punishment. He gets upset because he can't understand something and then mom leaves. He might easily start to think that expressing anger is bad and that if he does it people will leave him, because that is what happened with his mother.

The attachment to a parent is extremely important to children. If expressing anger means that the relationship with mom is going to disappear, what is the child going to sacrifice? The anger or the attachment to mom? It is likely going to be expressing the anger because the attachment to his mother is stronger and more vital to his existence than the desire to express his anger. Losing his mother would mean losing the care and support he needs, and thus life itself, at least in his limited understanding as a child. So if he thinks authentically expressing his anger will lead to losing mom and the care and support that comes with her, the child will almost always choose to suppress the anger.

The problem is that this then becomes an unhealthy coping mechanism that actually hurts the child in future situations, and unless it is worked through, it will continue on into adulthood. When the boy grows up, he may find that he hides things from his partner because he is scared she will leave him if she discovers what he really thinks. Relationships are built on trust, so you can imagine how this would affect future relationships for the boy.

Imagine another scenario. There are two children born in a similar place at a similar time. One of the children has a mother who is sensitive, caring, and responsive to his needs.

When the child cries, the mother is quick to respond and gives him the type of loving care he needs. The second child has a mother who is distant and disengaged. When he cries, she is slow to respond, if she responds at all. This child does not get much attention or loving care. Even though these two children were born into similar circumstances, the relational experiences they had would likely shape them in dissimilar ways. When these two children got older, it is likely that they would have much different experiences with relationships. The first would likely have good relationships because he would have confidence that he was loved and that his needs would be met because this is what he experienced during his childhood. The second would likely develop a certain level of neediness or dependence because he subconsciously believes that his needs will not be met. He might gravitate to people who take care of him in an inappropriate way, in areas he should be caring for himself. On the other hand, he might avoid relationships altogether because he wouldn't believe anyone could actually care for him. Maybe he would try to become self-sufficient or refuse to accept help from others. Regardless, whatever behavior he exhibits, it isn't likely to be healthy.

This is also one of the reasons marriage is the ideal relationship for raising a child. When a child has both a mother and a father in their home, they are more likely to receive the love and attention that will foster a secure attachment style. The parents can support each other and aren't solely responsible for the child's needs. They can work together and trade off taking care of the child. The child also has the opportunity to receive both masculine and feminine attention, which is important for learning how to interact with people of both sexes. If a child is raised solely by one parent, they may have problems with people who are the opposite sex of that parent. For example, a child raised by her mother may have secure attachments when it comes to her female friends, but may have major issues when dealing with men. Having both parents provides a more balanced perspective. The child can feel the nurturing presence of his mother and the strength and protection of his father. This is extremely important for child development.

There are a lot more details involved in attachment theory and if you are interested, feel free to look into it further. The reason I'm bringing it up here is because it shows that the relationships we have in one part of life can greatly influence how we will act in other relationships. It shows that the way people treat us actually affects the way we view ourselves. In regards to our current topic, something that will greatly increase a person's confidence is having secure attachments. Ideally, these develop in early childhood through our relationships with our parents and family members. However, many people never get that privilege. As we've stated earlier, a lot of people grow up in dysfunctional homes, sometimes even experiencing neglect or abuse. Don't worry. If that is the case for you, it doesn't mean you are doomed to a life of low confidence and failed relationships. There are other ways to develop secure attachments such as surrounding yourself with good friends or developing a close relationship with God. Let's explore this a little more so that you have a map for navigating secure attachments.

CHAPTER 16

FRIENDSHIPS

Just a little earlier I said that you were going to need a lot more than me telling you about your value a few times in a book in order to truly believe it and develop confidence from it. This belief in your inherent value needs to become deeply rooted in your heart and in your mind. You need to believe you are valuable on a core level. You need to expect that you are going to be loved and cared for. Otherwise you won't be able to trust anyone, and without trust, your relationships will never flourish. Without trust you will never be able to make a sincere and total gift of yourself, which is necessary for you to truly love someone. So how do you develop this deep confidence in your value and dignity if just hearing it said to you a few times isn't going to do the trick?

One of the ways you can become more confident in this truth is by developing good non-romantic relationships.

Basically, go make some good friends. Good friends are people who are going to be able to remind you of your value when you start to doubt it. They are going to be a consistent voice of truth and love in your life. They will show you love, which will help you to believe that you are worthy of love. This doesn't mean they simply affirm you all the time. Good friends are not "yes men." No, good friends will affirm your value, but they will also tell you the truth because not all things should be affirmed. A good friend is someone who desires what is actually good for you, not simply what makes you feel good. Sure, they will encourage you when you are on the right path, but they will also call you out when you are headed down the wrong path. This doesn't mean they criticize you constantly. It just means they will challenge you to become a better person, and as you become a better person, you will gain confidence.

One way to tell the difference between people who don't care about you and friends that are being critical in order to help you is by noticing whether they build you up at the same time they challenge you or not. If they simply point out your flaws without giving any constructive feedback, they probably aren't the types of friends we are talking about. Again, good friends will challenge you, but only to help you become a better person. These are the types of friends you want in your life. These are the types of friends that will help you to become a more confident person.

Maintaining good friendships will also provide the added benefit of having a full life outside of any romantic relationships. This will give you more freedom as you begin to date and it will protect you from becoming too attached to people too quickly. You will have the security of knowing that if anything goes wrong with the person you're dating, you always have these friends to fall back on. Good friends might even help you navigate your dating relationships by giving you advice and feedback, and this can insulate you from serious heartbreak. They will help you become stronger in your social skills without having the high stakes of a romantic relationship putting pressure on you to perform. They will help you practice trust and vulnerability. They will give you opportunities to work through conflict. On top of all that, having good friends will also make you more attractive in itself. It shows others that you have at least a basic grasp of social skills, and it can be a good sign that you aren't a total weirdo or psychopath. If other people like you, it signals that there must be something likable about you.

Having friends can also alleviate some of the worry a mate might have of you putting too much pressure on them to become the center of your life. It will make you seem less needy, and in effect it will actually make you less needy. Plus, having good friends will provide you with people to ask questions about the people you date. They might be able to see flaws or red flags that you can't see with the blinders of early infatuation on. If you have good friends and they don't like the person you're dating, there might be a good reason for it. This doesn't mean you should rely solely on the opinions of your friends. It's more like using them as a compass to tell you if you're heading the right direction or not.

There are so many positive things that come from having

good friendships that I would suggest that you don't even begin thinking about dating until you have a solid group of good friends. Notice that I said good friends. You can have friends that aren't good. Whether they can actually be called friends or not, I don't know. The point is that you should consider the quality of your friends. If you have friends that are jealous, make you feel rotten, always look at themselves as better than others, peer pressure you into doing stupid things, or are lazy and apathetic, you should consider whether these are people you want to keep in your life or not.

Just as good friends can help you in dating and other parts of life, bad friends can be toxic. They can make you doubt your identity even more, and subtly cause you to think that you are worthless. Bad friends are often insidious in their toxicity. They will be kind to you when they want something from you, and then become a devil when they don't need you anymore, causing you to feel chaos and confusion. Many people don't even realize they have bad friends. They are so used to toxic relationships that bad friends just seem like the norm. They make excuses for their friends' bad behavior and justify the poor treatment they receive. We all have a deep desire to be loved and so we are often more willing to endure abuse and manipulation than risk the pain of feeling isolated and alone. It may be scary, but if you have toxic or abusive friendships, it is vital that you root them out of your life. They are not going to give you the solid unshakeable confidence you need to become attractive and in fact may end up sabotaging your chances at having a good healthy dating relationship.

This doesn't mean you can't associate with people who aren't perfect. They don't exist. But you shouldn't put up with abusive negative people. Your core group of friends should be people who are virtuous, loving, and unselfish. These are the kinds of people who will lift you up when you fall. They will help you to understand that you are valuable by treating you as though you were. It's vitally important that you surround yourself with good friends.

CHAPTER 17

MENTORS

Even though I just hyped up how important it is to have good friends, they won't be able to provide you with everything you need. Finding good friends is a great start, but there are some things that simply can't be learned through friends alone. Another type of relationship that is vitally important isa mentorship. Mentors are people who have greater wisdom, experience, or knowledge than you in a given area of life. They can come in many forms, from coaches and teachers, to coworkers and employers. Even books like the one you are reading can be a form of mentorship, though I do suggest finding real life mentors as well.

Mentors are important because they can help guide you along the right path and avoid pitfalls. They are people who have already made the mistakes so you don't have to. They can give you advice directly or you can learn by watching them. One of our favorite ways to learn as humans is through imitation.[10] A mentor is someone you can learn from by imitating them. This doesn't mean you should try to be somebody else. That would go against everything I've been talking about so far. It simply means that you can see how someone who is an expert does the thing they are an expert at and figure out what makes them good at it. Then you can apply those skills to your own life. This can dramatically increase the speed at which you learn or accomplish a task. There is no more precious resource than time, and learning from mentors can save you massive amounts of it.

Our parents are usually our first mentors, but as you should know by now, not everyone has good parents. Parents are supposed to be the main people we learn from as we grow up, but what do we do if our parents were bad parents or not involved in our lives? This is where mentors can be incredibly valuable. They can fill in some of the gap, teaching us the things we never received from our parents.

Regarding the subject of this book, finding people who have had successful relationships can be a great way to improve your own relationships. For example, if you are looking for a romantic relationship, find a couple who has a successful marriage to mentor you. This can be an excellent way to learn about dating and relationships. They can help you understand what a healthy relationship looks like. They can tell you what attracted them to each other and what kept them together. Having a mentor in this area is going to dramatically improve on what you are learning in this book. Even better, you could ask your mentor if he or she would be willing to discuss it with you. Having a mentor will help you to apply it all.

Mentorship doesn't just need to be for the purpose of learning about relationships either. There are so many other areas of life that mentors can help you with. An employer can help you improve your work. A coach can help you to improve in your sport or become a better leader. A pastor can help you grow closer to God and understand how He is speaking to you. And as you improve in these different areas of life, you should become more confident, which again, will also improve your social life. These things all build on each other. Sure, there are things specific to relationships that will help you in your dating life, but the goal should be to become an altogether well-rounded person. This is what will make all of life better. Simply having a good dating relationship isn't going to solve all your problems or make you feel fulfilled. It is only one piece of a many-pieced puzzle. Finding mentors is going to help you in a much more holistic way, while simultaneously improving your ability to relate to others.

So how does one get a mentor? A good place to start is by looking at the people and places that are already familiar. Is there someone at your work who seems like they know what they are doing? Do you play a sport? Are you part of a church? Who are the people in these places that you admire or look up to? Once you have an idea of who these people are, invite one of them out for coffee or lunch. Ask them thoughtful and interesting questions. Offer them free help with something you want to learn about. After you start to build a relationship, you can ask them to be a mentor. Make sure you give them an idea of what you are expecting. You could suggest something like, "I'd like to meet with you once every other week to learn more about your work," or "Can I call you when I have questions about this?"

If you struggle finding a mentor in this way, you could try a more structured approach, such as hiring a coach or signing up for a class. Some settings even have mentorship built in, such as jobs that pair you up with a mentor. That shows how valuable mentors are to people. There are many different avenues to pursue mentorship, and it doesn't hurt to have multiple mentors. The point is that you should have them. They are going to be of great benefit to you and really help you grow as a person.

CHAPTER 18

THE GOSPEL

So far we have looked at the value of having good friends and mentors, which is indeed enormous. However, there is another relationship that far exceeds the value of both of those, or any other relationship for that matter. The most important relationship of all is a relationship with God. For some of you this will seem like a no brainer and for others this will seem like something for people with no brains. I get it. Not everyone believes in God and not everyone has experienced Him. I spent much of my own life ignoring God. Guess what? That was also the period of my life when my relationships were the most dysfunctional, and I was the least satisfied with life.

A relationship with God is the primary and most fundamental relationship we can have, for God is the source of all life. He is the very One who created you! If you aren't on board yet, please try to suspend your disbelief for a little while and keep an open mind. This section of the book has an incredible amount of potential to completely transform your life. If after reading it, you decide it's not for you, that is something you are free to do. Love is a free choice. You can continue on and pretend like you didn't hear anything. You can even toss the book out the window, light it on fire, or drag it to the trash bin on your desktop. However, that would be extremely heartbreaking to me. As someone who genuinely cares about you, it would be incredibly sinister for me not to warn you that you would be making the worst decision of your entire life. Without God, you are not only going to have a harder time with relationships, you are going to experience eternal damnation in Hell. I'm not saying that because I relish in scaring you. It's simply the way things are, and I want to make that clear. It's like you are trapped in a burning building on the brink of passing out from smoke inhalation, and I'm trying to show you where the phone is so you can use it to call the fire department before you pass out and it's too late. I can't encourage you strongly enough, please try to read this portion with an open mind. You might find an immense hidden treasure more valuable than you even believe is possible.

Developing a relationship with God is the number one most impactful thing that I've experienced in my own life... by a long shot. There isn't anything else that has even come close. That's because there is no one who can get to the deepest roots of our struggles except God. There is no one else who understands you in the uttermost depths of your being. You could have the most brilliant team of doctors and therapists that exist and they wouldn't even be able to scratch the surface of understanding you the way God can. He is the One who designed you. He knows your thoughts, fears, traumas, joys, and desires. This whole book has been about relationships, and we've touched on why they are so important to us as humans, but now I want to go a little deeper.

One of the main reasons God created us was so we could have a relationship with Him. That's why relationships are so fundamental to our existence. This next quote is from the Bible. I hope you will be able to see the deep truth contained within. If you read it with an open mind, you might discover amazing insights into life and existence.

"So God created man in his own image, in the image of God he created him; male and female he created them. And God blessed them. And God said to them, "Be fruitful and multiply and fill the earth and subdue it, and have dominion over the fish of the sea and over the birds of the heavens and over every living thing that moves on the earth." And God said, "Behold, I have given you every plant yielding seed that is on the face of all the earth, and every tree with seed in its fruit. You shall have them for food. And to every beast of the earth and to every bird of the heavens and to everything that creeps on the earth, everything that has the breath of life, I have given every green plant for food." And it was so. And God saw everything that he had made, and behold, it was very good. And there was evening and there was morning, the sixth day." (Genesis 1:27-31)

The first man, Adam, and the first woman, Eve, originally existed in a blissful relationship with God. God entrusted them with everything. There was no pain, no sickness, no weariness. But there was about to be a test.

"And the Lord God commanded the man, saying, "You may surely eat of every tree of the garden, but of the tree of the knowledge of good and evil you shall not eat, for in the day that you eat of it you shall surely die." (Genesis 2:16-17)

The only rule God gave man was to not eat the fruit of the Tree of the Knowledge of Good and Evil, or else Adam and Eve would die. Seems pretty simple, right? Adam and Eve had everything they needed to be content. One type of fruit shouldn't have been a big deal. Yet, when you think about it, this is a situation we are often confronted with as humans. Have you ever been in a situation that was going great and you should have been content, yet there was something you didn't have and it was hard to turn your attention away from it? Sometimes we even use the expression "forbidden fruit" to describe this type of temptation. We seem to have a deep inclination to desire what we can't have. This is speculation, but it could have been what Adam and Eve were experiencing. Let's keep reading to find out what happened.

"Now the serpent was more crafty than any other beast of the field that the Lord God had made. He said to the woman,

"Did God actually say, 'You shall not eat of any tree in the garden'?" And the woman said to the serpent, "We may eat of the fruit of the trees in the garden, but God said, 'You shall not eat of the fruit of the tree that is in the midst of the garden, neither shall you touch it, lest you die.'" But the serpent said to the woman, "You will not surely die. For God knows that when you eat of it your eyes will be opened, and you will be like God, knowing good and evil." So when the woman saw that the tree was good for food, and that it was a delight to the eyes, and that the tree was to be desired to make one wise, she took of its fruit and ate, and she also gave some to her husband who was with her, and he ate. Then the eyes of both were opened, and they knew that they were naked. And they sewed fig leaves together and made themselves loincloths." (Genesis 3:1-7)

Bam! The first broken relationship in human history. The crafty serpent tricked Adam and Eve into eating the fruit of the Tree of the Knowledge of Good and Evil. Notice that Adam and Eve didn't immediately die. Rather, they brought death into existence. They broke trust with God and therefore broke the relationship they had with Him, and since He is the source of all life, if the relationship with Him is broken, then life can no longer exist without death. Adam and Eve also brought brokenness into their own relationship. Where shame had not existed, it now came into being. And being our original ancestors, we inherited these broken relationships with God and with each other, as well as the propensity to do evil, which is called sin.

Think about your own family history. Are there any dysfunctional patterns of behavior you learned or inherited from your parents or other relatives? This is why it is so difficult for us to have healthy relationships to this very day. Even with the best teaching out there and being brought up by great parents in a loving home, you and I are still going to suffer pain and brokenness in our relationships to at least some degree. It is impossible to avoid. Our broken relationship with God is even worse. Our human nature has been corrupted by sin, and without a cure, this brokenness has eternal significance. Have you ever lied? Have you ever stolen anything? Have you ever looked at another person with lust? Those are all sins against God's law, and sin leads to death. However, there is good news. This brokenness, this curse that was brought on by Adam and Eve, was reversed. "For the wages of sin is death, but the free gift of God is eternal life in Christ Jesus our Lord." (Romans 6:23)

You see, when Adam and Eve broke their relationship with God, it created an infinite gap. God is perfect and even the slightest sin or imperfection cannot be found in His presence. That means a sinful human can do nothing to restore their relationship with God. It would take an act of infinite value to do so. Fortunately for us, there is someone who was able to perform this act of infinite value, God Himself. God became one of us in the person of Jesus Christ. He lived a perfect, sinless life. Then He offered that very life as an act of love and redemption for us by dying on a cross. Through this act, Jesus showed us that the greatest love is a sacrificial gift of self, He showed us that suffering is not meaningless, and He actually paid the ransom for our sins, restoring our relationship with God and saving us from eternal damnation. He then rose from the dead 3 days later, proving that death had been defeated! This was confirmed by dozens of witnesses, including His 12 apostles, all but one of whom (who was exiled) were murdered for proclaiming that Jesus had risen from the dead. By rising from the dead, Jesus confirmed that His claim to be the Messiah was true and He opened up a way for us to have eternal life, no more held down by sin and death. All we have to do is repent of our sins and believe in Jesus Christ and we will be saved.

"For God so loved the world, that he gave his only Son, that whoever believes in him should not perish but have eternal life." (John 3:16)

It might be hard to believe, but pay attention to your heart right now. Is anything stirring inside? Is there a subtle feeling that this is true? I realize that it might seem a little far-fetched if you've never heard this story before. On top of that it is hard for me to tell it in a way that captures the magnitude and depth of such a story in such a short amount of space. It took me almost a year to read the Bible just one time, and that was while faithfully reading it every single day. That's also part of the beauty of it though. Learning what's needed is so simple a child could understand with only a few minutes of teaching, while at the same time there is enough here that you could dive in for years on end and still find new things. I'm still learning and discovering new truths years after deciding to follow

Jesus. If this section has stirred up your curiosity even a little bit, I would encourage you to get a Bible and read the story for yourself. That is really the best way of getting to know God and the story of humanity.

The main point I want to get across in this section is that restoring your relationship with God through faith in Jesus Christ is incredibly important. The original source of our broken relationships with others comes from a broken relationship with God. If you want your other relationships to turn out well, it is necessary to heal this original broken relationship. It's at the very heart of everything. The sins we cling to are often the very things that cause so much of our pain. I won't say that turning to God suddenly makes your life easy, full of puppies and sunshine. It doesn't. There are many hard things you will still have to face. But it is worth it. You will experience peace, joy, and freedom. You will find fulfillment, and experience healing in many of the areas you have struggled. It will blow you away to realize what is possible, and ultimately you will get to live eternally with God in a state of bliss that is not even fathomable in this life. Please consider this chapter with sincerity, and even feel free to say a small prayer asking God to reveal if it's all true. If you've never prayed, just speak out loud as if you were talking to a friend or relative and ask God what's on your heart. You could say something as simple as, "God, if this is true, please help me to see it." I believe you will hear an answer to that prayer.

CHAPTER 19

OTHER WAYS TO BUILD CONFIDENCE

So far we've talked about becoming more confident through building relationships that will help you develop secure attachments, affirm you in your value and dignity as a person, and support you in all the other areas of your life. If you have trustworthy people in your life, you will likely feel more secure and this will manifest itself as confidence. Having all the relationships we've mentioned so far is going to be a huge factor in your level of confidence, but there are other ways to boost it as well. For example, reading this book in itself should boost your confidence. Why? Because you are actually growing in knowledge and proficiency about something, and that is of real value. You are increasing your capacity to offer value to the world. You are increasing your capacity to offer your unique gifts to others.

Basically, if you believe you are capable of something, you will be more confident. Greater competence equals greater confidence. This can be a competence regarding just about anything, not just dating and relationships, yet it is still possible for it to impact your relationships even if that is not the thing you are directly growing more competent in. For example, you might learn how to play an instrument. That is a skill that is not directly related to relationships, but it can still help you grow in confidence, which could have an indirect positive effect on your relationships. It's almost as if that confidence in playing an instrument adds to your overall confidence, kind of like a character trait in a video game adds to the character's overall abilities. It also wouldn't hurt for you to be able to serenade your mate with music.

If you want to become more confident, become more competent. Learn a new skill or master one you have already begun learning. As I have already stated, it doesn't matter what it is. If you want to focus on relationship skills directly, I will be going over some of them in more detail later on. There are definitely some skills that will both help your confidence and be directly useful in the realm of relationships. For example, learning to read body language is going to help you in relationships more than learning computer programming will. Still, learning computer programming could make you more confident overall, and it isn't a bad thing by any means. The point of this section is that you are growing more competent in something and thus growing more confident. Again, if you do want to improve in things that will apply directly to dating and relationships, that's great. But as far as the current point is concerned, it's not necessary. The goal is simply to help you understand that becoming more competent will make you more confident. The next part will be about the mindset you should have when learning or doing things.

CHAPTER 20

MENTAL STRENGTH

As I write this it's almost midnight, I've had a long day, and I'm totally exhausted. Writing is just about the last thing I want to do right now. I'm so tired I don't even know if I'm making sense, and I will probably have to go back and edit this later on. However, that is precisely the reason I'm doing it. Greatness doesn't just come through a flash of inspiration. You don't just get an idea and all of a sudden become successful. Sure, the inspiration part might come in a moment, but then you have to actually put in the work to make it a reality.

Consistency is what builds greatness. Ask anyone who is a master at something, whether it be a sport, an instrument, or a business, and they will tell you that it took hours, days, and even years of work to get to the level they are at. They will also tell you it was well worth it. Contrast that with people who win the lottery. These people may experience an immediate change in their financial situation, but what usually happens next? Most of them don't even know what to do with the amount of money that was just dropped in their lap, and they often end up in worse situations than they were already in.

Things that are gained easily are hard to appreciate. Things that you've poured blood, sweat, time, and tears into are much more satisfying. This can be applied to so many different situations. Is the fast food burger and fries or the nice home cooked meal going to make you feel better? Is a text message that says "luv u" or a well thought out letter going to be more meaningful? Is a one night stand or a loving marriage going to be more fulfilling? In just about any situation you can think of, the things that take time and energy are the things that are worthwhile. So before you go for the quick and easy route, think about how your decision will build up your life in the long term.

This doesn't mean you should never do something that is fun or even something that is easy. However, there is massive value in choosing to do hard things, and doing them consistently. Maybe it means prioritizing the difficult stuff and making sure it's done before you allow yourself to relax. Maybe it's about learning to enjoy the process. Oftentimes the reason we settle for quick and easy things is because we just want to get to the outcome. We want instant results. We don't want to wait. Yet waiting is another key aspect to all this. The ability to delay gratification is one of the key characteristics that is found among successful people. Patience is a virtue. If you can learn to be consistent, enjoy the process, and be patient, the results might take longer to get, but they will be infinitely greater and more satisfying when you get there. This is the kind of growth which will bring core confidence.

Get Comfortable with Rejection

"The master has failed more times than the beginner has tried." (Stephen McCranie) Going along with this idea of doing what is difficult with consistency is another idea, becoming comfortable with rejection and failure. No matter what you are trying to accomplish, there are going to be times of rejection and failure. If you aren't prepared for it, your progress may be interrupted and even stopped altogether. Rejection and failure can be crippling. They can feel horrible and plant seeds of doubt. That is, if you don't know how to handle them. It is possible to push through rejection and failure, and even thrive in the midst of it. Choosing to embrace these things from the beginning will give you a massive advantage. When they inevitably show up, you won't be caught off guard. You will be able to recognize them as a sign of growth.

One of the reasons it is so important to be grounded in your identity, is that it will give you a solid foundation when the winds of rejection and failure assail you. They won't be able to shake your core confidence because your core confidence won't be based on success. It will be based on the solid foundation of faith in God and knowing the value of your life. Being grounded in your identity is massively helpful here. However, there are other things to help you embrace rejection and failure as well. For example, anyone who has gotten good at sales will tell you of the numerous cold calls they had to make and how they were rejected many many times. Doing something like this will sting a little bit at first, but eventually you will become more comfortable, and at some point you will likely cease dreading rejection or failure. Purposely exposing yourself to the risk of rejection and failure is difficult, but still easier than encountering it unexpectedly. By choosing it up front, you will condition yourself to it and be better equipped for those unexpected situations. Don't let rejection or failure stop you from going after your goals. Learn to embrace it. This will give you confidence and it will allow you to take more risks. You will not fear rejection or failure. You will not allow these things to dictate your mood. You will remain solid through any situation.

CHAPTER 21

ALWAYS TELL THE TRUTH

The next thing I'm going to tell you is huge, and it will have a massive impact on your level of confidence. Always tell the truth. That's it. It might sound simplistic, but it is massively important because lying will totally undermine your confidence. When you lie, you subtly say to yourself, "The truth about who I am isn't good enough." Furthermore, having confidence in something means you are able to trust it. If you are always telling lies, you will see yourself as untrustworthy, and if you are untrustworthy, you will not have confidence in yourself. On the other hand, if you are honest and authentic, you will have confidence in yourself because you know you are going to act in accord with the truth. You can trust yourself.

When it comes to relationships, trust is foundational. You can't have a good relationship without trust. When you tell lies, other people won't trust you, and even if they don't realize you are lying, you won't even be able to trust yourself. This type of distrust leads to self-loathing. Think about it. Do you like being around people who are untrustworthy? Do you like them? If you don't like untrustworthy people, but you know that you yourself are untrustworthy, then you will inevitably start to dislike yourself. If you always tell the truth, you will be able to trust yourself, and you will at least have that aspect of liking yourself going for you..

Telling the truth will also free up your mind from having to remember the things that you would have to remember when lying. You won't have to remember the details of a story because you can simply state what happened. You won't have to worry about inconsistencies when telling people about yourself. This extra mental capital can be extremely valuable. It can relieve stress and help you listen better. There are an entire multitude of benefits to telling the truth.

People will also be able to connect with you better because of your authenticity. Most people don't like fake people. They are untrustworthy. Telling the truth is a simple way to grow in confidence and foster better relationships. It might not be as easy as you think though. Sometimes telling the truth requires saying things people don't want to hear. Sometimes it requires sacrificing advantages or benefits you would be able to get through being dishonest. It means being vulnerable about your weaknesses and letting people see your faults. Telling the truth can be extremely difficult. However, it is well worth the effort. In a world that is full of liars, you will stand out as real and authentic. It will help you become even more grounded in your identity, and you will actually be able to like yourself, knowing that you are doing your best to do the right thing and live with integrity.

123

CHAPTER 22

TAKE CARE OF YOURSELF

Another thing that can help you become more confident that might sound pretty obvious, but is also commonly neglected, is taking care of yourself. That's right. I know it might sound silly, but taking care of yourself is a simple and effective way to improve your confidence. When you value something, you take care of it, and so by taking care of yourself, you are subtly letting yourself know that you are valuable. Now, what exactly do I mean by taking care of yourself? It will likely vary from person to person, but there should be at least something you do to take care of yourself. Maybe it's brushing your teeth twice a day. Maybe it is dressing up a little nicer. Maybe it's creating a budget. Maybe it's simply allowing yourself to rest. Try to notice if there are any areas of neglect because these can signal where you need to improve on taking care of yourself. If you notice you are constantly fatigued, maybe you need more sleep. If you have a lot of acne, maybe you need to wash your face more often. If you are overweight, maybe you need to eat healthier and begin an exercise routine.

There are many things you can do to take care of yourself, but I would suggest beginning where the biggest deficits exist and with the things that are easiest to implement. These are going to be the areas with the most potential for growth and are also going to be the most meaningful for you. Little changes can make a big difference in these areas. For example, if you already go to the gym 4 times a week for an hour and a half at a time, adding 10 minutes of exercise to your daily routine might not change things that much. However, if you never exercise at all, adding 10 minutes of exercise per day will create a massive change for you. So start with those areas of your life that have been most neglected.

Fitness and Nutrition

Since we are on this subject, let's talk about fitness and nutrition. You might think, "What in the world do fitness and nutrition have to do with relationships? I came here to learn how to socialize, not get in shape." It's true that fitness and nutrition aren't necessary for having good relationships or social skills. However, that doesn't mean they don't matter at all. It would be unjust of me to say nothing on the subject. There are many benefits to exercising and eating well that will directly translate into more success in your social life.

For one, staying fit and eating healthy takes discipline,

which will help you grow in virtue. We talked about the virtue of temperance for example. In order to eat healthy, it will mean denying yourself pleasurable foods for the sake of eating what is going to fuel your body and cause it to work well. That requires temperance. Another virtue we talked about is fortitude, which is the courage to continue under stressful conditions or when something is difficult. Working out is a great way to increase your fortitude because it literally requires you to do something difficult and painful over a long period of time. Staying fit is not something that happens after one workout. You have to do it over and over again without giving up. Hopefully, you can see how both of these practices will increase your virtue, which I have already highlighted as both something essential for having healthy relationships and something that will make you more attractive.

Fitness and nutrition are also a one-two combo on increasing your confidence. For one, they will both make you look more attractive. Fit people simply look better. Why is this? We are wired on a biological level to desire people who are more likely to survive and pass on our genes. Physical fitness signals this on a very deep level because it shows that a person is strong and healthy. Back when humans existed in hunter gatherer societies, that could mean the difference between life or death. People desire things that will increase their chances of survival and a healthy mate is one of those things. Eating well will assist in creating an attractive physique and give you energy to work out, as well as make your skin look good, which will signal that you are healthy. Exercising regularly will help you lose fat, gain muscle, and keep your body strong. When you start to see yourself look better externally, this will increase your confidence internally. This doesn't mean your value comes from looking good. Ultimately, what kind of person you are is what really matters. However, there is an objective increase in attractiveness that comes from looking healthy, and you should know that it exists.

Working out and eating healthy will also increase your confidence by showing you that you can do difficult things. As you succeed in these disciplines, you will be reaching new goals repeatedly. When you succeed at one thing repeatedly, it will give you confidence that you can succeed at other things too. Therefore, fitness and nutrition are both great ways to boost your confidence. Again, you don't need either of these things to be a confident person. This book contains plenty of tools for that, which don't require working out or eating healthy. Look at these two things as bonus tools that are also very practical. For example, you might struggle with understanding how to change your thought process because it is more of an intellectual thing, but fitness and nutrition are straightforward physical things you can do and start implementing right away. One person develops their mind, another person develops their body. They both grow in confidence.

You don't have to become a bodybuilder or go on a vegan raw food diet. Start with something that is a small step in the right direction. Maybe it's just taking a walk around the block every morning. Maybe it's replacing one processed food with a fresh fruit or vegetable. If you are farther along with either of these things, then make it appropriate for where you're at. Eventually you will get so accustomed to this way of life that it is simply what you do. I have been working out steadily for at least 15 years now. At this point, it's just what I do. Nutrition has been a little more inconsistent for me, but I definitely notice I feel better when I eat healthy. I try to ask myself whether what I eat is going to make me feel better or worse. If you can look at your food as fuel, it makes it easier to make healthy choices. Whether you implement this stuff or not is totally up to you. Just realize that it will make you feel better, increase your confidence, and help you to have better relationships, even if it is in a secondary way.

Sleep

One other aspect of taking care of yourself that is extremely important is getting enough sleep. It's something many people seem to struggle with. When a person doesn't get enough sleep, it can lead to all kinds of problems. For example, they won't be able to function at their peak potential and they won't be able to perform tasks as long as a fully rested person would be able to. Not getting enough sleep can also mess with hormonal balance, anxiety levels, and bodily health.[11] Sleep is where our bodies rest, recover, and heal. During sleep our muscles repair themselves and our brains process information and experiences. Getting the sleep your body needs might take more time, but it will improve your performance so dramatically that it is well worth it.

There are a couple considerations regarding sleep that

I will cover here. First, the most important thing is that you get enough sleep. The ideal average amount a human needs is probably around 8 hours, though it varies from person to person. Try to figure out the right amount for you to be well rested. You want to get enough sleep without oversleeping. Some people will propose ideas like waking up at 4:00am to get an early start on things. This is not necessary. What matters is the amount of sleep you get. If you want to wake up at 4:00am, that's fine, but you will probably have to go to bed by around 8:00pm. If you'd prefer to go to bed at midnight and wake up at 8:00am, that works just as well. You are getting the same amount of sleep. Find times that work well for you. Once you find a time, it's important to keep it consistent. You don't want to bounce back and forth from waking up at 4:00am and waking up at 8:00am. Try to get in the routine of going to bed and waking up at the same time every day. Our bodies are set up for rhythmic patterns of sleep.[12]

The next consideration is that you want to get good sleep. There are different levels of sleep and the deepest ones are important for many of our biological processes. Here are some ways to improve your quality of sleep. First, stay off electronics for at least an hour before you plan on going to bed. The blue light from screens can mess with your brain, causing it to stay in "awake" mode. On top of that, if you are feeding your mind information right before bed, you may be more likely to keep thinking about that information, which will make it harder to fall asleep. Another thing that can help you sleep better is setting up the environment where you sleep. Make sure it is as dark as possible, set the temperature to something that is comfortable, and keep it quiet if you can. Regarding temperature, cooler is usually better, though you don't want to feel like you are freezing either. Finally, try to avoid caffeine late in the day.

All of these strategies should help you get enough sleep and stay well rested. This will improve the performance of your body and mind, and cause you to feel better all around. If for some reason you don't get enough sleep from time to time, it can be helpful to take naps if you're able. You probably don't want these to be any longer than 45 minutes. That's enough time to give you a boost without getting into a really deep sleep. Being well rested is super important for staying healthy and having an optimal amount of energy. It will improve your mood, and it should make it easier for you to feel confident.

CHAPTER 23

BOUNDARIES REVISITED

Another thing that is related to taking care of yourself, that will also boost your confidence, is maintaining good boundaries. We've talked about boundaries already, but they are also important in the current context. By maintaining boundaries you subtly signal to yourself that you have value, and this will inherently boost your confidence. Maintaining boundaries means you have standards. You don't just go with the flow. There are things that you say "no" to because you know they would be harmful, and you know that valuable things are worth protecting.

When you maintain boundaries, other people will start to respect you more, which could also improve your confidence. When others show you respect it is easy to interpret that as a sign that you are valued in some way. If you believe you are valuable you are going to have more confidence. Taking things even a little beyond boundaries, which are mostly there to protect you, it's also good to develop your own likes and interests. Discover what your preferences are and stick to them. It's good to maintain an open mind and be willing to try new things, but if there is something you've tried and know you don't like, don't pretend like you enjoy it because you think someone else will like you more if you do. It's nice to share common interests with people, but most people aren't looking for someone who changes their preferences based on the situation. When you voice your opinions and preferences, it helps other people trust you. They can see that you are likely being honest. It shows that you are comfortable with who you are. You aren't willing to act a certain way to please others.

This is where the advice to "just be yourself" begins to make sense. Being authentic is an extremely attractive trait. It also gives you a certain freedom. Trying to guess what people think you should like or dislike is exhausting. You have to think about and analyze all these decisions that are totally unnecessary to even consider. By knowing your likes, dislikes, and opinions, you can simply speak what's on your mind without having to think about it. So take the time to discover what you like and dislike and then stick to it. It will help you develop a greater sense of self and help you to become more confident.

Neediness is the biggest killer of attraction. No healthy person wants to feel like they are totally responsible for your happiness. It puts a ton of pressure on them, and will likely make them run away from you. Don't get me wrong, people want to feel appreciated for being in your life, but that's different from neediness. There are not many people who want to feel like they are totally responsible for you, unless they themselves struggle with neediness, and if that's the case, any relationship you form with them will likely be dysfunctional.

From your perspective, you shouldn't need anyone to complete you. You are complete already. You are whole already. Relationships are 1 + 1, not ½ + ½. When you come from a place of security, especially in your identity, this will be attractive to others. They will want to be around you. It also gives you freedom because you won't be dependent on others to provide your happiness. Now you might be thinking, "Is there any way to tell if I'm acting needy or not?" One sign that you are coming from a place of neediness is hurrying. That may seem strange, but let me explain.

When you hurry, it's often the case that you're seeking something outside yourself. It shows that you're not content with where you are right now. Someone who is secure in their identity doesn't need anything outside of what they already have. This doesn't mean they don't have any goals or ambition. It simply means that they can be content with enjoying the process, rather than being dependent on an outcome that may never be achieved. They can work hard, yet be detached from any outcomes. Their value comes from who they are, not what they have or do. This is the opposite of neediness.

Someone who is needy will always be searching for something external to themselves. Often this ends up being sought out in other people. When that happens, attraction dies. Desperation ensues. Getting rid of neediness is key in becoming attractive to other people. Relationships, especially romantic relationships, are going to go a lot better when others are attracted to you, rather than you chasing them from a place of neediness. Think about it. If you are chasing something, what does that mean? It means that the thing you are chasing is running away from you. How do you think that is going to work in a relationship? Do you want people to run away from you? Attraction is called attraction for a reason. It is all about becoming a person that others will be drawn to. It's about providing value to other people, rather than trying to take something from them. This can be applied to any kind of relationship; romantic, friendships, business, etc. It's simply the natural way humans work.

I've personally experienced both neediness and attractiveness in myself and others. I used to be the neediest person you could imagine. This was due to childhood trauma, societal conditioning, bad role models, and a host of other things. Regardless, it was the way I experienced and engaged with life. I was constantly seeking something outside myself to fulfill me. Often this was girls. I would see all my friends being successful with girls and I would get jealous. Whenever I tried to initiate something with a girl I seemed to always get rejected or ignored. When I did have success in starting relationships, they were always short lived. The girls I dated would seem to be into me initially, but then lose interest rapidly. What was happening? The biggest problem was that I would quickly become needy. At the beginning of relationships, it might not have been as apparent, but after a couple of weeks it would always come out, which is another example of why you need to develop your identity before utilizing social skills. In these situations, I was able to use social skills initially, but I was not able to keep it up because I wasn't grounded in my identity. I would start to place my value in the relationship, rather than realizing it came from who I was as a human. I began to need the relationship in order to be happy. Again, no one wants to be responsible for someone else's happiness.

On top of that, the neediness wasn't even for these girls as people. Often it devolved into me needing them for what they could offer me physically or emotionally. I needed them to gratify my desire for physical pleasure, and thus turned them into objects for use. I needed them to gratify my desire for emotional connection, and thus turned them into vessels I could dump my problems on. It's no wonder these girls would change their attitude towards me so quickly. The ironic part was that the more I was rejected, the needier I would become, thus getting rejected even more. It was a vicious cycle that at times led to great dissatisfaction in my relationships. I yearned to be desired, but it came off as desperate.

Desperation is not a good look. It makes it seem like you have no other options. Even if someone is interested in you, if they think that you are just taking whatever you can get, it forces them to have to look at themselves as not having much worth. On the contrary, if the other person perceives that you have a lot of options, choosing them will likely make them feel like they must be extremely valuable. For example, when learning to play sports, kids will often choose captains to pick who is going to be on each of the teams. The captains take turns picking who they want to be on their team. Usually, the most athletic people are chosen first with successively less and less athletic people going each round, the final picks basically coming down to who is still left. If you've ever been in this situation, you know that the greatest fear was being picked last because this meant that you were expected to be the worst player. You were the least valued.

It's the same with relationships. If someone is one of many options, and you choose them, it will make them feel extremely valuable. If they are the only option, it will make them feel like they are of almost zero value. People may even choose to not be in a relationship at all over being in one where they have to admit they are not valuable. People don't want to be picked last in captains, and they don't want to be your last resort in relationships. Neediness is one of the biggest indicators that you don't have many options, and if you stop acting needy, you will often find that more options begin presenting themselves. By communicating that you don't need someone, they may even start to feel like they have to win you over and then actually start trying to do so.

There is a major caveat here. This should NOT be looked at as a trick to manipulate people. I'm just describing the dynamic that happens with neediness in relationships. You genuinely should try to cultivate security in your identity. You should not need anyone else to make you happy. If you try to fake it in order to get a girlfriend or boyfriend, or even just to make friends, eventually these people will figure out that you really aren't as secure as you made yourself seem. You will also likely feel insecure in the relationship and worry about the person leaving you, which in effect is being needy. By trying to fake it, you actually end up doing the exact opposite of what you are trying to do. That is not going to result in any healthy relationships. Learn to be content without seeking anyone else's validation, and eventually people will start showing up in your life.

Another aspect to this is learning to let go of people who simply aren't attracted to you. Stop wasting your time trying to change them. It's hard, if not impossible, to control who we are attracted to. It's like forcing a small child to eat broccoli when they want nothing to do with the stuff. You might get them to eat it, but there is no way to make them like it. If a person isn't attracted to another person there is virtually nothing that can be done to change that. If you've ever had someone you weren't attracted to come onto you, you understand what I'm talking about. It's very uncomfortable, and you wish the person would leave you alone. This doesn't mean they're a bad person or that they're unattractive to everyone. Your preferences don't dictate the status of other people. It simply means you are not attracted to the person.

It can be helpful to understand the fact that some people just aren't attracted to each other and that's ok. Keep this in mind when you are looking for a mate. If you show interest in someone, but they don't reciprocate, it is probably a good idea to move on. Why chase someone who isn't attracted to you? There are millions of other potential mates out there. This doesn't mean you won't occasionally see resistance from people you are pursuing. No one is going to be totally on board with everything you say all the time, and if they are, that might be a red flag in itself. Even people who are attracted to you are going to disagree with you and show some resistance from time to time. However, if someone is attracted to you, they are going to at least give you some indication that's the case. They might tease you, but then touch your arm. Or they might disagree with you, but smile as they do it. They aren't going to stonewall you in every instance. If that's happening, the person is probably not attracted to you, and you are wasting your time trying to pursue them.

Even if you can somehow convince someone who isn't attracted to you to date you, it's probably not going to be a healthy relationship and it will likely end poorly. A good example of this is when beautiful young women date older rich men because they buy them stuff, and the women get to live the luxurious lifestyle they desire. They may get their material desires met, but they are not relationally fulfilled. Those kinds of relationships often end up with one of the two parties cheating on each other or having some other kind of catastrophic breakup happen. There was never attraction there in the first place, and the people were fooling themselves.

Here I need to point out that attraction isn't the only thing that matters in a relationship, especially physical attraction. Two people can be very attracted to each other and also have a horrible relationship. That's where all the other stuff I've talked about such as boundaries and virtue come into play. Here I simply wanted to emphasize the idea that you shouldn't settle or waste your time with someone who isn't attracted to you. There are millions of potential mates out there. Spend your time on those who are just as interested in you as you are in them. Don't try to force someone into liking you. Find someone who actually likes you. You will be much happier that way. The ironic thing is that sometimes when you stop trying to pursue the people who don't like you, later down the road they will change their mind about you. Perhaps they realize the value you brought into their lives or they see you growing and changing into someone who is more their type. Whatever the case, please don't settle for someone who doesn't have the same interest in you as you have in them.

CHAPTER 24

ARTIFICIAL CONFIDENCE

When you are trying to be more outgoing and improve your social life, there are some pitfalls that are easy to fall into, especially in modern culture. I will go over these in more detail later. For now, there is one area I want to suggest setting a boundary in because it is closely related to confidence. Your boundaries will likely look different than mine, and it is ok to have different ones. However, the one boundary I've made that I will encourage you to also take up is to avoid drugs and alcohol. Let me explain why, especially in the current context of increasing confidence.

Drugs and alcohol can be a tempting way to loosen up and become more confident in social interactions. They often lower inhibitions and cause people to take bigger risks. I've even called alcohol "liquid courage" from time to time in my earlier years. The problem with this is that drugs and alcohol only provide an artificial kind of confidence. It's a shortcut that might work temporarily, but ultimately will lead to greater dysfunction and heartbreak in your relationships. It's worth putting in the time and energy it takes to actually learn the skills to excel in social situations, rather than using drugs or alcohol as a crutch. They may help you get over fear initially, but in the long run they make things much worse. They can cause you to waste money, act belligerent, and kill ambition.

It is ok to have a drink or two socially if you're old enough, but if you're relying on drugs or alcohol to help you become more social, you are going to regret it. The route you're going to want to take is to develop social skills and confidence without the aid of these things. This will help you to change and become confident at a much deeper level. You will be able to talk to people in any situation instead of just when you are intoxicated. This is extremely important. In the past I relied so much on drugs and alcohol for my social confidence that I began using them in strange contexts. It began with wanting to talk to girls at parties or bars, but eventually I started using these things for just about any situation I would have to be social in. I would get intoxicated before going to a sporting event, a movie, or an art gallery. I even remember getting messed up for at least one family gathering. I didn't feel comfortable being myself in any situation where I was sober. This led to some major dysfunction. Learning social skills without the aid of drugs and alcohol will give you so much more freedom in your interactions with people. If you see someone you want to talk to, you will be able to do it, no matter the context.

Another thing to consider is why you would even want to use drugs or alcohol. If you really think about it, you might be surprised. Often drug and alcohol use starts with peer pressure. Giving into peer pressure might get people to like you initially, but ultimately they are going to lose respect for you and you're going to lose respect for yourself too. It's similar to what happens if you change your preferences based on what you think people want you to like or dislike. It makes you come across as weak and unsure of yourself. If you are being peer pressured into drinking or drug use and you stand your ground against it, others will respect you for that, and you will feel a sense of strength. This will be another source of true confidence for you. And even if it pushes some people away, the type of people it pushes away might not be the type of people you want around you anyways. I'm not saying you should start viewing yourself as better than others because you don't use drugs or alcohol. What I'm saying is that people who can't enjoy using those things themselves without pressuring you to join in, probably don't have your best interest in mind. If people can enjoy those things while simultaneously accepting your decision not to, there is no reason you can't be acquainted with them.

CHAPTER 25

FILTERING

When one's confidence is restored or realized, this should cause the person to filter themselves less. Does this mean that they just blurt out random obscene thoughts like someone with Tourette's Syndrome? Not at all. What it means is that the person acts in congruence with what they are thinking. For example, if I see a woman I want to talk to, I will go and talk to her. I won't stop myself by filtering. In that situation the filtering could come in many different forms. It might be that I make excuses such as telling myself that the woman is busy or that I don't want to bother her. It might be that I fear cultural pressures. Whatever it is, if it's stopping me from expressing what I am actually thinking in my mind, it's filtering, and it's not allowing me to be my authentic self. In reality, those filters are things I've created in my own mind. They are barriers of my own design. This is good because it means that everything needed to tear them down exists within my power. I can learn to break through these filters and live more authentically. There are many ways to do this.

A good first step could be to start paying attention to your thoughts and actions as you go about your day. You want to do this so you can identify where you are filtering yourself. When do you feel comfortable being yourself? Where do you feel pressure to act a certain way? For example, you might feel comfortable when you are around friends or family, so you might be very relaxed in that setting. You might say things you wouldn't say in other situations that are less comfortable. Oftentimes we end up fighting a lot with our family members because we feel comfortable around them, and this isn't necessarily a bad thing. It could lead to better resolution of conflict, at least if you handle it well and there isn't any lingering resentment. You will have expressed what is going on in your head, and then you can let it go instead of bottling it up inside, which is what causes resentment in the first place. It's an example of how not filtering things will lead to better relationships.

On the other hand, a situation many people feel more pressure in is when they're at work. Maybe you'll notice yourself filtering yourself when you are around your boss or another coworker. You might be afraid that you will get in trouble if you say the wrong thing. There are certainly social structures and norms that you should follow to some degree. However, many people are censoring themselves in ways that aren't necessary. You want to be aware of this. When you're aware of the ways you're censoring yourself, you can begin to address them.

There are many possible reasons for censoring. Often

it's a program or belief someone received as a child that has stuck with them. For example, maybe someone yelled at you for talking too loudly when you were a child and you developed a tendency to speak softly or not speak at all. Maybe you confronted someone about something and they yelled at you, and now you avoid confrontation. If you notice yourself filtering yourself in a certain way or in particular situations, you can think through your past and see if there is something that happened in a similar way.

For example, let's say you notice that you're censoring yourself when you're at work. You could try to think of things that happened when you were at school or with authority figures, and see if there was anything that happened that might be causing you to act the way you are today. Maybe you realize you asked a teacher a question and they scolded you for it. Once you realize this happened, you can try to figure out the false belief or response and replace it with a better one. You might realize that you adopted the belief, "I shouldn't question authority because I will get in trouble." You could then say to yourself, "I got in trouble when I asked my teacher that question, but my teacher was wrong to respond in the way he did. It was his negative response, not my question, that caused the problem. Asking questions is a good thing. It helps me live in the truth. If I get a negative response, it isn't always my fault."

You have to start rewriting the script of the things you say to yourself. When you correct the script, it will come through in your actions. Another way to fix filtering problems is to change your actions in order to change the script. Let's continue with the same example of asking questions to people in authority. If you notice yourself filtering in this way, you could intentionally do the thing that you think will result in a negative response. You could purposely come up with a question to ask someone in authority, and see how they respond. If you ask someone a question in a respectful way, they are most likely going to respond in a respectful way. That's something you can probably understand on an intellectual level. It's your subconscious you need to overcome. When you actually experience a positive reaction, it will help you to see that the script you currently have is faulty on that subconscious level. So, if you ask your boss a question and your boss responds positively, that means that your script of, "I shouldn't question people in authority because I will get in trouble," isn't always true. Therefore, by intentionally doing something that goes against your current script, you are providing a reference for rewriting it.

Let's examine one more example of how this works from start to finish. We can use social anxiety, which is relevant to the topic of this book. Let's say you want to get better at approaching strangers and talking to them, but you have extreme social anxiety. You notice that every time you want to approach someone, you chicken out and filter yourself. When you examine your past, you realize that you approached some kids on a playground one time and they threw sand at you. You also realize that your parents weren't around to support you and let you know that you were ok, and it was really the kids that were being mean. You didn't have the unconditional love of your parents to fall back on after this traumatic incident. You were all alone. Then you realize that these things that happened in the past have caused you to adopt the belief, "Strangers don't want me to approach them, and they will hurt me if I do." You might realize that this belief is irrational on a conscious level, but you also realize that you really do believe it on an unconscious level. Before you were aware of this belief, you didn't understand why you shy away from talking to strangers, but now that you know of the false belief, you have a reason to approach people that will hopefully give you enough courage to at least attempt it. Now it's time for action.

Start small. Walk up to a stranger and give them a compliment. Even though your subconscious will be repeating your false script to you, you can remind yourself of the truth that, "Most people like being talked to." Let's say it gives you enough courage to do it and so you walk up to someone and give them a compliment. It is highly likely that you will get a positive reaction, and at the very least it is unlikely that you will get a negative one. If you do, you will at least walk away knowing that you are still alright, and you will feel good that you had the courage to at least attempt something. If you get a positive reaction, you can tell your subconscious, "See, that belief that people will hurt me if I approach them is false." You have now actually experienced that people like it when you approach them. From there you keep doing it until the lie is proved false and you believe the truth on an unconscious level.

As you do this more and more, it should get you to the point where you can strike up conversations with people in all kinds of situations. If you find that you can't even get over that initial anxiety to give a stranger a compliment and get the process started, recruit a friend to encourage you and hold you accountable. You could even do something like give your friend a $20 bill or whatever might be slightly painful to lose, and tell them not to give it back to you until they see you give a stranger a compliment. This will be an added layer of motivation. If your friends are willing, you could also try role-playing the situation. Ask your friend to pretend they are a stranger. Try approaching them in the way you want to approach a real stranger. Ask your friend to respond positively. Consciously you will realize that this is only a role play, but your subconscious experience will be that of having a stranger respond positively to your approaching them, and you will get practice. Remember, increased confidence often comes from increased competence. You will want to move to real interactions as quickly as possible, but this is another tool you can use to reinforce the positive beliefs about yourself and rewrite the script.

Also, I used the example of approaching strangers to illustrate how this process works, but you could do it with any situation. Maybe you notice yourself filtering yourself with police officers and realize you had a bad experience with a cop in the past. You can use the same process to stop filtering yourself around police officers. Figure out if there are any false underlying beliefs you have around police officers. Figure out what the truth is. Enter into a situation where you have to confront the lie. Rewrite the script. Just don't go commit a crime in order to have an interaction with a police officer. That probably won't reinforce anything positive.

I know all this probably sounds easier than it actually is. It will take some practice and you won't get it perfect every time. Push yourself as far as you can, but also give yourself grace. You don't want to start beating yourself up. As with most things, it is good to enjoy the process. Get help if you need it. Earlier I mentioned a bunch of people that can help you grow. Recruit friends to help. Hire a therapist. Find mentors. Having others to help you will cause you to grow a lot faster. The goal is to become authentic in what you say and how you act, so that you can be present and enjoy life. It is very freeing to feel comfortable with yourself as you really are.

CHAPTER 26

MEDITATION

One final tool I will share for becoming more confident is meditation. Meditation is helpful because it increases your ability to be present in whatever situations you end up in. Meditation is different from prayer. Prayer is having a conversation with God. Meditation is practicing the control of your thinking. Throughout our waking lives, we are bombarded with thoughts. These thoughts can be good, bad, or neutral. The ability to think is a great thing. It allows us to solve problems, it allows us to communicate, and it gives us the ability to carry out a number of different tasks. However, thinking can also be problematic. It can cause anxiety and worry if we are too focused on the future, and it can cause depression if we are too focused on the past. Generally, we are going to be more content if we are focusing on the present. Meditation is a way to do that.

Basically, meditation is training your mind to stay present despite the distracting thoughts that come in. This is harder than it sounds. A great way to start is simply to take a small chunk of time, maybe 10 minutes, and sit in silence with your eyes closed. Breathe deeply. As you sit, try to focus on your surroundings. What do you feel? What do you hear? If any thoughts come along, just redirect your attention back to the present moment as soon as you notice you've drifted. Meditation isn't about force. It's about letting go of your thoughts so they don't pull you away from the present moment. If you want, you can put on some calm instrumental music, or use an app or recording to assist you. Just beware of anything that tries to add a spiritual aspect to things. Meditation is about gaining control of your mind, not reaching some enlightened state of consciousness where you become one with the universe. As you meditate regularly, you will likely notice that you are able to stay present in other situations as well. This should decrease your anxiety, and help you be more confident in your social interactions. If you are in a stressful situation, use the skills you've built up in your intentional meditation time to focus yourself on whatever is happening in the present. You are less likely to filter yourself if you are in the present moment. You will better be able to listen to people because your mind will be less distracted with whatever thoughts are in your own head. I could go further in depth about meditation, but just a simple practice of 10-20 minutes per day is plenty to get you started. Just doing that is enough. Really, anything else might just overcomplicate things. Keep it simple.

CHAPTER 27

CONFIDENCE CONCLUSION

If you've gotten this far, you are well on your way to becoming a secure, confident person. I know it might seem like a lot of work, but it is absolutely worth doing. If you've already started, you probably have already noticed some improvements in your social life. It's hard to emphasize how important having confidence is when it comes to improving your relationships. However, there are still a lot of other tools available. Next I want to give you some of the practical skills you can start to use in your social interactions. When you combine developing deep core confidence with growth in your ability to communicate, you will supercharge your social life. You will develop relationships you didn't even think were possible. So get pumped as we dive in!

CHAPTER 28

INTRO TO SOCIAL SKILLS

Alright, the moment many of you have been waiting for, practical skills. Hopefully by now you've realized that knowing your identity and value, gaining confidence, and maintaining good boundaries are some of the most important parts of fostering good relationships in your life. Relationships aren't a formula. There are real people involved. You have to become the type of person other people would even want to be in a relationship with in order to have success. If all you do is drag people down, no one is going to want to be around you. If you are unable to present your true self authentically, then the relationships other people form with you are nothing more than an illusion. You are convincing people to connect with a fictional character that isn't you. Only when you have accepted your true self and have made the decision to live authentically are you ready to learn the practical skills. Otherwise they will just become part of the imaginary character you've made up.

So what are these practical skills? Social skills are all the external actions that contribute to any kind of social interaction. They encompass all the different ways we can communicate with each other. This can be very obvious stuff like the words we speak, or it could be more subtle, such as the facial expressions we make. Communication is often happening on multiple levels at the same time. A person may speak words that communicate one thing, position their body in a way that communicates another, all the while using frame control to communicate something else. Much of this stuff will just happen naturally if you aren't paying attention to it. However, if you work on these skills intentionally, it is possible to get better at them and communicate more effectively. It's kind of like breathing. Most of the time you don't notice you are doing it. Your body just automatically does it for you. However, if you pay attention, you are able to control your breathing. You can take deep breaths, you can take quick shallow breaths, or you can even hold your breath. The moment you stop thinking about it, your body will take over again. It works similarly with social skills. Take body language for example. When you are interacting with someone, your body is going to do something. It's not just going to freeze in place until you consciously think to move it. However, if you do consciously think about it, you can move your body to communicate something specific, such as waving your hand to greet someone. Due to there being so many layers of communication happening at the same time in a social interaction, you will want to avoid trying to incorporate too many new social skills at once. As you read through this portion of the book, try practicing one new thing at a time. You can certainly read about as many of the skills as you want. Knowing how things work is going to benefit you regardless of whether you practice specific skills or not. Just know that you will only be able to incorporate so much at a time. This stuff takes a long time to master. It would be foolish to try skiing down a double black diamond before you have even figured out how to get on and off a chairlift. Take it easy at first and don't get discouraged. If you stick with it, eventually you will improve.

The following things you're about to learn can be extremely powerful. If you diligently implement them you will probably start noticing more attention from the opposite sex and people just being more open to you in general. This is another reason why all of the info we covered on identity and what healthy relationships look like is so important. Anytime you have a powerful tool, it's critical that you know how to use it. Learning and using these external skills without a solid foundation would only reinforce the bad one. Thankfully, at this point you should have a rock solid foundation and be very secure in your identity. So with that, let's dive in.

CHAPTER 29

BODY LANGUAGE

The first thing we'll cover is body language. That's right! Your body actually speaks a language. It is able to express who you are and what you're thinking, even without words, and sometimes even *more* effectively than words. Have you ever interacted with someone who spoke words that indicated they were very happy, but something about them made it seem like they were actually sad? That's body language. I'll give an even clearer example. Can you think of a way to tell someone to stop without using words? That's right. Hold up your hand with the palm facing forward. That's another example of body language.

People who are excellent communicators understand body language. They can read it in others and they can use it themselves. As we've covered already, inner confidence is probably the most important thing when it comes to attraction. This is just another example where the inner work pays off.

Often good body language will follow if you have genuine confidence. However, it is still good to know what good body language looks like because we can use it to improve how we communicate, and it can help us understand what others are communicating to us. We can also use it to do things like foster confidence itself. Our minds and bodies are connected and sometimes when you are struggling with confidence, using good body language will work in the other direction to *make* your mind think you are confident. We can literally move our bodies in ways that will help our minds to follow. Some of these things will seem like very small nuances and maybe even trivial, but that is one of the awesome parts about understanding body language. Simple changes that are easy to implement can gain huge results. It can be tough to master body language, but the basic things needed to become more attractive should be pretty easy to do.

Posture

The first thing you can do to improve your body language is fix your posture. Stand and sit up straight with your head up and your shoulders back. It's as simple as that. There are a few different reasons good posture is important.

First, it makes you look more confident. It subtly tells people that you believe you have value. It makes you look bigger. It makes you look stronger. When you have good posture, people will take notice. Try it out sometime. Enter a room full of people with a slouched posture and pay attention to how they react. Then try it again. This time enter a room with your head held high and shoulders back, and again pay attention to how people react. See if you can spot a difference. Do people give you their attention? Do they themselves straighten up? It's easy to try. What have you got to lose?

Another reason that good posture will benefit you is that it will actually make you feel more confident. I know this might sound a little questionable, but it's true. By changing your posture to a confident one, you will begin to actually feel more confident. It will probably be a subtle change, especially at first, but there should be a difference. Again, our minds and bodies are connected. When you have your body in a confident posture, your brain will take that information and likely interpret it as, "I'm in a confident posture. I must be confident." If you train yourself to be in a good posture most of the time, this will have a cumulative effect and hopefully you will actually start to become more confident, simply from a slight change in your body position.

Maintaining good posture is simple, but it can be a little bit tricky to implement. You might find that you sit up straight, but then after five or ten minutes you have begun to slouch again. The key is to intentionally straighten up every time you notice yourself slouching. It might take days, weeks, or even months before it becomes your natural posture, but if you intentionally work on it, eventually it will become more natural and you won't have to consciously reinforce it as much. If you need to, you could even do something like set an alarm on your phone to go off at different times during the day and then readjust at those times.

One thing to watch out for as you are trying to fix your posture is becoming rigid and stiff. Sitting and standing up straight might cause you to tense up. You want to be able to maintain a confident posture while also being relaxed. When someone is stiff and tense, it is usually a sign that they are anxious and insecure. That won't make you look or feel confident. If you notice that you are stiff when you begin trying to fix your posture you can try to relax yourself in a couple of different ways. The first thing I'll suggest is tensing yourself up even more. I know, it seems counterintuitive, but hear me out. Try flexing every muscle in your body as hard as you can for about ten seconds. Then release them and let them relax as much as possible. Something about this contrast helps to loosen things up. This might work in some situations, such as when you are practicing your posture at home by yourself, but often when we tense up it is due to being in a social situation. If that is the case, then flexing all your muscles for ten seconds might not be the most comfortable thing to do. Don't worry. There are a couple of other things to try out. First, just take some deep breaths and slow down your breathing. Try to breathe in as if you were trying to suck the air into your feet. When you exhale, relax all your muscles as much as possible. That is a simple, quick way to release some tension. Another thing you can do is try to accept the tension. The tension may be there because you are under pressure, social or otherwise. If you accept the tension, it may relieve some of the pressure, and eventually help you to relax. Basically, just give yourself permission to suck for a little while. Often the tension we feel is a result of wanting or not wanting to be perceived in a certain way by others. Maybe you want to be perceived as cool and confident, therefore you put pressure on yourself to perform in a way that will be cool and confident. By allowing yourself to just suck for a little while, it may relieve that pressure, which inadvertently will actually make you more confident. Remember, the point of learning all these practical aspects of social interaction isn't meant to make us into an avatar of someone we aren't. They are meant to make us more confident in ourselves as we truly exist. The goal of all this is to help you to be your true self so that you can offer your unique gift to the world. This is about being able to embrace the person you were created to be.

Space

Another aspect of body language that is related to posture is taking up space. What do I mean by this? Let's think about it. Our bodies are the vehicle through which we are able to express ourselves. This means that the way they move and act in space reflects something about us. Think about this question. On average, do you think a big person or a small person is going to be more confident? Depending on the situation, it could go either way, but at least for me, my first inclination is to think the big person would be more confident. Someone who is big has strength and power. On a biological level, they are more likely to be at the top of the food chain. They are less likely to lose in a fight, and they are more likely to be successful in hunting, building, and providing. This doesn't mean that someone who is small doesn't have their own strengths. I'm simply trying to point out our instinctive perceptions as human beings. If you saw two bears wrestling in the wild, would you expect the bigger bear or the smaller bear to win? On a subconscious level, we attribute more confidence to those who are bigger.

This is something you can find in many parts of nature. Some animals have physical characteristics specifically designed to make themselves look bigger. Think of birds with colorful feathers that flare up, or the puffer fish, which puffs up like a balloon in order to prevent predators from attacking it. When a bear is running at you, the best thing you can do is spread yourself out, wave your arms, and shout like a madman. You try to make yourself look big so the bear will back off.

So how does this relate to social interaction? Some people reading this book might be naturally large, and that is great. However, some people reading this book are probably on the smaller side. That's great too. What I am talking about here is applicable to anyone. By expanding your body you can take up more space, thus making yourself look bigger, which inevitably will make you also look more confident. I know it might sound silly, but it's incredibly effective. If you examine the body language of successful leaders, they often take up a lot of space. This is why you will see great public speakers walk around the entire stage while they are speaking, sometimes even coming down to interact with the audience. They are taking up space. Maybe you can imagine the charismatic talk show host using all kinds of hand gestures to emphasize his jokes. He is taking up space. Taking up space will cause you to look more confident, and as with some of the other things, it will actually cause you to feel more confident as a side effect.

There are many ways to start implementing this kind of body language. I've already talked about maintaining good posture. You can also spread yourself out when you are sitting down, keep your feet slightly farther apart when standing, or walk around and move within the space you occupy. That last one could be on a stage if you are public speaking, but it could also be in places where the attention is not specifically on you. For example, you could do it at a party by walking around and talking to different groups of people. You still want to give people your full attention when you're with them. If you take this too literally, there is the danger that you will start wandering around without any purpose and it will look like you are lost. That is not what I'm talking about here. I'm simply saying that instead of standing in the same place all night, you allow yourself to use all of the space available to you.

Another body language tool to take up space is using your hands while you're talking. This will not only make you look bigger, it will help you emphasize the points you are making. Using gestures is easy to implement, but difficult to master. There are many nuances to the things you do with your hands that communicate differently. For example, if I am using a lot of big gestures, but have my hands closed, that could be a sign that I'm aggravated and on the verge of attack. Making those same gestures, but with open hands, may communicate enthusiasm or honesty. Both situations are similar examples of speaking with your hands, but they communicate very different ideas. For most situations, having open body language is going to be the most beneficial. Open body language means that you have your arms and legs outstretched and away from your body, and have your hands open. This communicates an authentic and welcoming presence. Closed body language communicates insecurity and signals that you don't want to be talked to.

This is actually a biological thing as well. The reason a person would have closed body language is to protect themselves. They cover up the most vulnerable parts of their bodies. Their heads are bowed down so their necks are not exposed, and their arms are drawn in so their heart and belly aren't exposed. Imagine a turtle retreating into its shell. This usually occurs when a person feels threatened, which means they would also likely be anxious. By putting your body in that position you are likely to communicate anxiety, and just like good posture can make you *feel* more confident, this closed body language can actually begin to make you *feel* anxious. Open body language communicates confidence because a person with this type of body language is making themselves vulnerable. They are signaling that they're not worried about an attack, which also implies that they're strong enough to defend themselves. Hopefully, you don't need to worry about people actually physically attacking you. I just wanted to point out that this stuff is wired into us biologically. Keeping all of these things in mind will help you to develop good body language.

This also isn't meant to be an exercise in puffing yourself up. It's simply meant to help you use your body to express who you really are. Again, that is why it is so crucial to understand the core concepts I have been emphasizing throughout this book. This body language stuff will create results in your social life, but unless you are strong in your identity first, it will only get you so far. When you have strong body language, people might try to test you to see if it is authentic or not. If you aren't strong in your identity, people will eventually figure out that it's only a show. That's not how you develop great relationships. You will only wind up with shallow ones. You can improve your body language in order to appear more confident, but it should be body language that truly expresses the character you have already developed internally. Again, as you practice these things you shouldn't expect perfection. These are tools to help you express yourself, not magic formulas to make you into a superhero. The way you use them will determine the results you get.

Eye Contact

Eye contact is perhaps the most powerful aspect of body language for bettering your social skills. Relationships are based on connecting with people, and the eyes are a part of the body that accomplish this in a powerful way. There is something about gazing into a person's eyes that connects people together. There is a feeling, a sense, that you get about another person by looking into their eyes. This can even be observed scientifically by studying what happens in the brain when people make eye contact. The social parts of our brain become active. These parts of the brain actually prepare us for connection with each other, therefore making eye contact with people should help you connect with them.[13] It should give you a sense of knowing who they are, and it will make it feel like you are known by them. For this reason, making eye contact with people can be very intense. If you aren't used to doing it, it may feel awkward or difficult. It may make you feel vulnerable. Yet, it's probably the simplest and most impactful thing you can do with your body to start forming deeper relationships.

There isn't much you need to learn to be able to make eye contact with people. It's pretty straight forward. Direct your gaze to another person's eyes. However, this doesn't mean it's easy. Making eye contact is so powerful that it can feel uncomfortable. There are a few things we can consider that will help us make better eye contact.

First, making eye contact with people doesn't mean you just stare people down to the point of extreme discomfort. This probably isn't a huge problem for most people. Unless you are already pretty confident, it's more likely that you aren't making enough eye contact with people as of right now. Still, you should at least be aware that it's possible to make others feel uncomfortable if you stare at them for too long. You want a balanced approach, not shying away from making eye contact, but also not burning a hole through someone as if your eyes were laser beams. A good method is to try and mirror what the other person does. Hold eye contact with them until they break it, and then look away until they look at you again, and then make eye contact with them again. This is a technique called mirroring, which we will examine in more detail shortly.

Another consideration regarding eye contact is that breaking it too quickly can be interpreted as submissive. For example, if you are looking at someone you find attractive, they catch you, and you immediately turn away, that is going to come off like you are fearful or unworthy of their attention. It implies that you feel shame for looking at them, or that you weren't supposed to be looking at them. It is better to maintain eye contact for at least a few seconds before diverting your gaze elsewhere. When you do break eye contact, try to do it to the side. Avoid looking down, which communicates insecurity. You also may want to give a smile as an indicator that you are friendly. Staring with a straight face can be perceived as threatening. Think of two boxers staring each other down before a fight. You probably don't want that.

Another consideration regarding eye contact is that it's a powerful tool to emphasize a statement. When you look people in the eyes as you speak, it gives your words a much greater impact. Pay attention to this because many people find it easy to make eye contact while listening to someone else, but have a much harder time maintaining eye contact while speaking themselves. If you can develop the skill of making eye contact as you speak into a habit, you will set yourself apart, coming off as very charismatic, and the more you can start maintaining eye contact with people in general, the more you will start connecting with them. Again, it's possible to make too much eye contact, but as I already noted, it's more likely that you aren't making enough. As you are learning this skill try to hold eye contact longer than feels comfortable. You could even try counting to 3 in your head. That might not seem like a long time, but it will feel like it when it comes to eye contact. It may be a huge challenge at first, but if you can implement it well, it will have a massive impact on your relationships.

Mirroring

Since I mentioned mirroring with eye contact in the last section, I will now go into mirroring more broadly. This is a technique that can be utilized using any part of the body, as well as speech. One way that people connect with each other is through empathy. Empathy is being able to relate to someone in the way that they are feeling. It's entering into another person's experience with them. Knowing that, mirroring is a great way to empathize with another person. Humans are creatures of imitation. The way we learn is by imitating others. Mirroring is imitating what another person is doing with their body or speech. If someone's arms are open and their head is held high, putting your own body in the same position would be considered mirroring. You move and use your body in the same way the other person does. How does this help you empathize with that person?

Remember that we are a body, mind, and soul composite. The way we move our bodies is an expression of what is happening in our minds and spirits. It also works the other way. If we move our bodies into any given position, this often causes our minds to think in a way that is congruent with our body. As I already mentioned, if we sit up straight, our mind may start to think more confidently, which is just one example of how this works. By mirroring and moving our bodies into the same position another person has, we can actually start to have similar thoughts and feel similar emotions to the ones that they have. This can help us enter into their experience and therefore empathize with them. You might not be consciously aware this is what you're doing, but it will happen. Keep in mind that this is not empathy itself. It is simply a tool to *help* you empathize with people. When you start mirroring other people, you might notice that they'll become more open to conversing with you and be more engaged in general.

I also mentioned that mirroring can be used in speech. The way you do this is by repeating back to someone what they just said. If they say, "I was walking my dog today," you can say back to them, "walking your dog," in an acknowledging way. This isn't meant to mock or mimic the person like little children often do when they play copy cat. Rather, it's meant to demonstrate that you are engaged with the other person. If you start paying attention, you will probably notice people doing this in conversations naturally. By mirroring what another person does and says, they should get the feeling that you understand them. This is what empathy is, and why mirroring can be so powerful.

Movement

Body language doesn't just involve the position your body is in. It also entails the way you move your body. Something you can do to make yourself look more confident is to slow down your movements. Often when someone is feeling anxious, they make quick jittery movements. These kinds of movements seem rushed. When you slow down, you are communicating that you are comfortable where you are. Animals provide some great examples of this. A deer or a rabbit has very quick jittery movements. They are always on the lookout for predators and need to be able to react quickly to escape them. This is not a bad thing. It's in their nature and it helps them to survive. However, it does show how quick movements are related to feeling anxious and uncomfortable. On the other hand, look at the lion. The lion moves very slowly in most situations. It's comfortable in its environment. Sure, it has great speed, but it preserves that speed for quick bursts used in hunting. It's not worried about anything attacking it. The lion knows its power.

Another lesson we can learn related to slow movements is becoming non-reactive. This is another way to show confidence. When you are slow to react to someone who tries to push your buttons or intimidate you, it makes it seem like you aren't threatened by them. It can also give you time to think in order to make a proper response. This can be in physical or verbal situations where things are tense. It shouldn't be confused with having slow reaction times. In many situations you do want to be quick to respond, yet remaining calm while doing so. For example, if there is a car accident, moving quickly and knowing what to do in order to help people is a sign of strength and confidence. This idea of non-reactivity mostly applies to situations of conflict with other people. It's also extremely difficult to learn. Unless you already have rock solid confidence, you aren't likely to pull this one off. It's not something that can be faked. Still, it's good to be aware of.

Moving slowly also isn't the only thing to consider when

thinking about body movement, and it isn't always even the best way to communicate confidence. A person can move too slowly. People who are severely depressed sometimes move extremely slow. For some people, the problem is that they're *too* stifled in their body movements. If this is the case for you, then you may actually want to exaggerate your movements. Make yourself bigger and more animated. Flail your hands around as you tell stories. Walk around purposely as you talk. Emphasize points with your hands. Smile bigger. Furrow your brow deeper. These things will make you seem more interesting and charismatic. It just depends on your personality and the situation.

In order to see what different movements look like and specifically how you look using them, try out different ones in the mirror, or record yourself talking on camera and then watch it. You could even do one recording where you don't move at all and then compare that with one where you act very animated. Also keep in mind that a lot of this will happen naturally if you are confident, which is another reason why the foundational stuff is yet again extremely important. Sure, it's good to practice your body movements, and know what you're doing, but unless you have true confidence in the first place, it won't be nearly as powerful as if you did. On the flip side, if you already have confidence, these movements can be a tool to accentuate your personality. You can even begin to hone and refine them. You can master them and incorporate them in a variety of places from public speaking to family dinners. You can also pay attention to how other people move their bodies and use this to try and get a read on how they are feeling.

Someone's movements can give you a lot of good information about a person. Are they threatened? Are they anxious? Are they confident?

This can be applied to people you are interested in dating as well. Certain body movements can be indicators that someone is interested in you or disinterested in you. A soft touch, playing with their hair, or a simple smile can be signs that someone is attracted to you. Closed body language, keeping distance, or pointing their feet away from you can be signs that a person is not interested in you. Knowing this can be helpful information because when you're trying to find a mate, it helps to pursue people who are mutually interested in you. Not everyone will be and that's ok, but it's good to know so that you can move on to someone who is. Body movements can help you with that.

CHAPTER 30

VOICE TONE

What you say isn't nearly as important as how you say it. Let me be clear, I'm not saying that truth in speech doesn't matter. What I mean by this is that people are going to connect with you based on how you make them feel. You could have the most perfectly crafted response to everything a person says, but if you say it in a way that communicates that you're nervous, the person will sense it and it won't have any impact on them. On the flip side, you could say the dumbest nonsense ever, but if you say it with total confidence, you will probably create some sort of connection with the person you're talking to. I've seen people walk up to someone, speak literal gibberish, and somehow captivate the person they approached.

The way things are said is much more important than the words themselves, at least for how it makes other people feel. If you have good things to say and you develop a strong delivery for those things, you are going to be on another level. However, the place to start is in the delivery.

There are two main parts to developing good delivery for speaking. The first is developing inner confidence, which should be familiar by now, and the second is knowing what attributes of speech make you sound better. Since we've already taken a deep dive into how to develop confidence, I won't go over that here, but I will briefly talk about why it's important. Between confidence and technical skills, confidence is by far the more important aspect of speaking. As you've probably realized by now, this is the case with just about every part of social interaction. I just want to point it out again regarding speaking. When someone speaks with confidence, others notice. What I mean is that there is no way to fake confidence here. Either you have it or you don't, and if you don't, it's going to be an uphill battle. Still, you shouldn't let this stop you from at least attempting to talk to people, and others may appreciate that you have the courage to speak even though you're nervous. People just aren't going to connect with you in the same way they will if you speak from a place of confidence. If you can develop confidence and let it show in your speech, you are going to get massively great results when you talk with people. It's so important that it can actually override any technical skills you could learn.

For example, normally it's more attractive to speak with a slow, deep voice tone. However, if you have confidence, you can speak in a high pitched whine and still get good results. Again, it's one of those things where having both is going to be ideal, but there is a certain superiority of confidence over skills when speaking. If you aren't at a place of confidence yet, it would be good to go back and work on the things that will help you to develop it. In the meantime, practice your speaking anyways.

Now I'll get into the technical stuff. There really isn't a ton of information you have to know, but mastering these things is difficult. The main things that are going to improve your speech are slowing down, using a deeper voice tone, and pausing. Slowing down, similar to body movement, is going to communicate that you are calm and confident. It shows that you are thoughtful and aren't rushed. Deeper voice tone builds on that. Keep in mind, this doesn't mean you should change your voice so much that it sounds comical or try-hard. It should be a subtle change using your natural voice. One way you can practice this is by recording yourself and then playing it back. Pausing builds suspense. It makes the person listening to you wonder what you are going to say next. You can pause right before making a major point in order to emphasize what you're going to say. You can also pause in the middle of sentences, to keep people engaged. When pausing, be careful not to let anyone interrupt you. Always finish your thought, before deferring to someone else. Otherwise, you will start to lose respect. This doesn't mean you have to dominate the conversation. Simply finish your sentence, and then let the other person take the spotlight. Another thing you can consider is the way you end your sentences. Try to examine the way you speak and listen to see whether you use an upward or a downward inflection at the end of sentences. An upward inflection means that the pitch of your voice rises at the end of sentences, and a downward inflection means that the pitch of your voice lowers at the end of sentences. An upward inflection communicates insecurity and a downward inflection communicates confidence.

If you master these speaking skills, you can take it another step further and practice dynamics. You may have heard this term if you have ever learned how to play an instrument. Dynamics refers to the cadence and volume you play with or in this case, speak with. A way to become a more charismatic speaker is to vary those things up. For example, you could start speaking in a very soft, quiet voice to draw people in, and then once they are hooked, you say something loud and with energy. This variation makes things a lot more interesting, and will engage your audience more. Working on dynamics is a higher level skill though. You want to get good at the basics first, and once those are natural, then you can shift your attention to dynamics. At first you might have to be very intentional, and then as you practice, it will become so natural that you forget you're even doing anything. However, you can always improve, so it's not a bad thing to intentionally practice, no matter what skill level you're at.

CHAPTER 31

HUMOR

When learning how to interact with other humans, it can be easy to make everything super serious. It makes sense. If something is important to you, then you are going to want to give it your best. This isn't a bad thing, but it can sometimes lead to taking things *too* seriously, which ironically will make your interactions bland and thus not as effective when trying to build relationships. So how do you avoid this? One way is humor. "But what if I'm not funny?" Don't worry. You don't have to be a stand up comedian to inject more humor into your interactions. There are some simple tricks you can use that will help.

The first one is to laugh at other people's jokes. This will make them feel good and build rapport. Make sure not to do it in a way that's fake or makes it seem like you're trying to suck up to them. You want to laugh at things because they are genuinely funny. However, sometimes it helps if we are intentionally looking for those funny moments. Also, we often stifle our laughter. We suppress it out of fear that we will be perceived a certain way. The confidence work and emotional healing you have done up to this point should help, and is the true cure for this. However, there are a couple of other ways to get yourself to laugh more, even if you don't need the emotional healing part.

Keep in mind that this is more about allowing yourself to laugh than it is about forcefully making yourself laugh. Doing it forcefully will come off awkward and make it seem like you're trying to impress people. Try to notice things that you actually find funny and let down any restraints. Often, once you begin to laugh, the laughter just grows and grows. Other people, who may be stifling their own laughter will suddenly feel more comfortable letting it go and you will all feed off each other.

If you want to take it even further, you can build on other people's jokes. For example, if someone gets into a funny role play and starts speaking in an accent, you can start speaking in a different accent and play along. This is a surefire way of getting the entire group laughing. It will make you more likable because you'll be making everyone feel good, and it will help you loosen up and not take things so seriously. It also creates camaraderie through experiencing a funny situation together, which you can even make jokes about later on by calling back to the situation.

What do you do if you can't seem to find anything funny or you just struggle with laughing in general? One idea is to figure out something you do find funny and watch it before you go out. Is there a TV show that makes you laugh? How about a stand up comedian? Try to find something that genuinely makes you laugh and watch it or listen to it before going to do something social. There are relational circuits in the brain, which when turned on, allow us to connect with people on a deep level. Humor is one of the ways these circuits can be turned on, so by finding something that makes you laugh before you go out, you are setting yourself up to be in a state that helps you connect with others relationally.[14]

As I briefly mentioned above, if you really struggle with being able to laugh, you may have some emotional healing to do. Sometimes traumatic experiences from the past can prevent us from expressing ourselves fully. This isn't the section to learn how to do that, but just note that it might be the reason it's difficult for you to laugh.

If you can't laugh because you're in a bad mood, a little trick is to totally exaggerate whatever you're feeling to the point that it becomes absurd and then laugh at that. For example, if you are sad you could say, "I feel like a sad little boy and I want to cry a river of tears so deep it could drown a fish." Make sure to say it with a pouty face and whiny voice tone. Use everything you have to exaggerate it and see if it doesn't make you laugh. Slowly you will probably start feeling better and then you will be able to genuinely laugh at other things too.

Another part of adding humor to your interactions is learning how to laugh at yourself. This one is huge! If you can laugh at yourself, you will be unstoppable. Not only will it make you more likable and help you to enjoy life more, it will make it hard for anything negative to ruin your day. Imagine someone throws an insult your way. If instead of getting mad and trying to defend yourself, you embrace the insult and laugh at it, it will totally disarm the other person and project major confidence to anyone witnessing the interaction. It shows that you aren't worried about what other people think. It shows humility by displaying that you don't think of yourself above others. It shows that you are comfortable in your own skin. The benefits of learning to laugh at yourself are massive.

For instance, it will allow you to take bigger risks in your interactions with others because if you say something stupid or make a mistake, you can simply turn it into a joke and laugh at yourself. This doesn't mean you try to make yourself look stupid. It just provides a way of dealing with mistakes that should give you more courage to try things. It's like playing hockey with pads versus having no pads. If you don't have pads, you might be willing to step out on the ice and play, but if you have pads you are going to try much more risky moves. You might skate faster, dive after pucks, or check other players. Without the pads you wouldn't do these things because you are more likely to get injured. Being able to laugh at yourself gives you the protection you need to take bigger risks in your social interactions. And since we are talking about humor, laughing at yourself is also one of the easiest ways to inject more humor into your interactions. Learn to laugh at yourself.

Notice that none of the techniques to inject more humor into your interactions I've mentioned so far are things that require you to actually be funny. That's because this isn't about getting laughs like a stand up comedian would be looking for. It's about loosening up and not taking things so seriously. It's about actually improving your social interactions so that you can build better relationships. That being said, it doesn't hurt to actually learn how to tell jokes. Learning how to joke around can make interactions more fun and it can be very attractive. It takes a clever and quick mind to make up jokes on the fly. I'm not going to try to teach you too much here, partially because I'm not that good at it myself, but know that it can be a valuable tool if you decide to learn how to do it. I would suggest watching stand up comedians, who actually know how to be funny, and imitate them. You could also try taking an improv class at a local theater.

I will mention one thing to be careful about here. Jokes can easily turn into insults, especially if you are trying to tease someone. Playfully teasing people can be a great way to build attraction or simply connect with them, but it can also go wrong quite easily. Playfully teasing someone has to be done in a certain way. Many people will fall into the trap of insulting others, which will do the opposite of what you are trying to do, which is build better relationships. A good rule of thumb to avoid this mistake is to make jokes that make other people look good, and if they are at anyone's expense, that person should be you. Unless it is completely obvious that you aren't insulting people, it could even be a good idea to avoid teasing types of jokes altogether, at least until you get really good with humor overall.

The other side of this coin is that you also want to be careful not to say things that come off as flattery. Don't make jokes that elevate someone unless you actually admire the thing you are elevating them for. Otherwise it will come off as try-hard or condescending. Try to be honest whenever you are making jokes. Actually, always try to be honest. The goal here is to be funny, not to mislead people. I've typically stayed away from a lot of pranks simply because they are often dishonest and involve outright lying to people. They often rely on deception. For example, a typical childhood prank we did as kids was to point our fingers like there was something interesting to see and then say, "Made you look." It might seem harmless, but practicing how to lie is not going to help you in any way. In reality it can subtly undermine trust, which is foundational for relationships. If a joke requires that you lie to make it, skip that joke. These types of jokes might get a laugh, but it will be at the expense of trust. There are plenty of ways to be funny that don't require dishonesty. In fact, sometimes the funniest thing is just stating an obvious truth that no one else is willing to state. That's actually what a lot of stand up comedians do. They say uncomfortable truths in a funny way. It's why it is so easy to resonate with them. Falling into dishonesty or disrespect when trying to learn how to tell jokes can be super easy, so try to be aware and audit yourself to see if what you're about to say is honest and kind. If there is even a little doubt, it is better to skip it. This book should be helping you to become a person of integrity. Maintain that integrity even in your jokes.

Here are a couple of other tips to improve your jokes. First, like anything regarding communication, be totally confident in your delivery. Even if it is a cheesy dad joke, if you deliver it in a way that makes it seem like you expect people to laugh, they probably will. If they don't, well, then simply laugh at yourself. If you tell the best joke ever, but you are unsure of yourself, you will likely feel dumb afterwards, even if people laughed at it. If you focus on amusing yourself regardless of what others think, it will likely lead to you being funnier and feeling better.

The next tip is to emphasize your jokes with as many of the tools available to you as possible. Use exaggerated body movements. Use props. Create characters. Use very specific language. I'll give an example for that last one. Instead of saying something like, "I ate a bag of chips," you could say, "I devoured an extra large bag of flamin' hot cheesy Doritos!" The extreme descriptiveness makes things more interesting because people often don't talk like that in day-to-day interactions. Use anything at your disposal to make your jokes more dramatic. This will not only make you funnier, but it will help your communication skills all-around. Hopefully, you are now equipped to spice up your conversations with a little added humor.

CHAPTER 32

STORYTELLING

Something related to but slightly different than joke telling is storytelling. Stories can be humorous, but they can create a lot of other emotions as well. They can communicate drama, sadness, anger, joy, and love. They can communicate your values or display your character to people. Plus, people connect with stories. That's why children ask to have books read to them before bed. That's why public speakers often start with stories. That's why millions of people regularly watch movies and TV shows. Before those things existed, people often passed down their values and beliefs through stories in the form of oral traditions. It is wired into us to desire stories. If you can learn how to tell them well, it will make you extremely interesting to people. Storytelling is one of the more complicated skills to get good at, but it is certainly possible, and usually worth the effort.

A good way to start learning how to tell stories is to do something like watch a movie or read a book, and then try and summarize it out loud in your own words. This will help you get better at recognizing what's important in storytelling without having to develop your own story to tell. That is something you eventually want to do, but having a sort of template to practice with can be helpful. As far as techniques go, there are almost as many as there are types of stories. Storytelling actually combines a lot of the social skills I've already covered. Things like voice tone and dynamics, body language, pausing, descriptive language, and speaking slowly can all be helpful when telling a story. You could incorporate props, use accents, or even involve other people.

An idea for practicing storytelling could be to choose one story and then tell it multiple times, each time focusing on a different skill. Another thing you can do is find a few of the best stories from your own life, write them down, practice telling them out loud, and then keep those stories in your arsenal to pull out whenever you are in a relevant conversation. That way you won't have to come up with something on the spot, and you will be able to focus on using skills and telling the story well.

When it comes to attracting a mate, think of stories that highlight something good about your character. Maybe you saved a puppy one time or refused to give in to a bully. This isn't about bragging to another person about how awesome you are. It's about realizing the good qualities you have and then picking stories that are both interesting and highlight those qualities.

When beginning your stories, a way to get people really

engaged is by starting with a hook. It could be very direct such as saying something like, "Do you want to hear about the time I put traffic cones all over my friend's yard?" It could also be more subtle such as dropping a comment like, "I had an obsession with yo-yos when I was younger," and then waiting for the other person to inquire further. The hook should be something that piques the interest of the other person so they ask you to share more. Once telling the story, role playing is a great way to get people engaged. You can play the different characters yourself, or even ask the other person to play one with you. Try to be animated and interesting. There are so many details we could continue to dive into, but that should be plenty to get you started. Storytelling is an awesome skill to help build relationships.

CHAPTER 33

COMPLIMENTS

Look for ways you can give people genuine compliments. Compliments encourage people and if done in the right way, will lead to people liking you more. There are a few things to keep in mind when beginning to compliment people more often.

First, you want to avoid flattery. This means you should only give compliments if you actually mean what you say. You should not have any hidden motives in mind, even something as simple as wanting a person to like you. If you give a compliment with the expectation of receiving something back, it is not a true compliment. Most people will instantly be able to sense that you are being fake. It might make you seem needy and insecure. Compliments that come from a place of strength are what you should be going for. They will be much more impactful that way.

Think of the difference in how you would feel if the salesman at a store complimented you versus how you would feel if your best friend complimented you. The friend probably would not stand to gain anything by complimenting you. They know you well, and thus they are not likely doing it to flatter you. The salesman, on the other hand, could easily be trying to butter you up to make a sale. This doesn't mean that a salesman can't genuinely give a compliment. It is simply meant to show that compliments mean more when they come from a place of sincerity. Flattery is the biggest trap you want to avoid when giving people compliments. You should be finding things you genuinely like about a person and letting them know it, which leads to the next tip.

Try to find things to compliment people on that are actually in that person's control. For example, if you say, "You have a pretty face," that is not going to be as meaningful as saying, "I like your hairstyle," and both of those will be far less meaningful than saying, "You really carry yourself with elegance, and your personality is captivating." Also, the more specific you can get, the better. Using the previous example, if you wanted to compliment someone's hair, you could say, "I like the way your hairstyle compliments your outfit." Even better, compliment people for things they have worked hard on to accomplish or for something about their character. Those are the most powerful compliments. They will mean the most to others, and they can actually encourage them to keep improving. Tell someone that you admire their artwork or that you like how they are trustworthy. Again, don't just say things to flatter people. Only give compliments about things that you actually admire. Just keep in mind that the more personal and the more effort it has taken the person to have whatever quality you are complimenting them on, the more the compliment will be appreciated and the more it will encourage the person.

Compliments are great because they are so versatile. They can be used to start a conversation, and they can be used as a way to soften healthy criticism. They can make people like you more, and they can encourage others. Don't be afraid to give people compliments. Just try to make sure you are being genuine. This will have the added effect of training your mind to find the good things in others.

Another aspect regarding compliments that I'd like to talk about is complimenting someone to other people. This can be extremely powerful. If the person is present, they will sense that the compliment is genuine because you are even willing to share it with others. It will also help them build better relationships with others themselves, because the people you shared the compliment with will now have a more favorable view of that person. If the person is not present, the compliment will still benefit them because others will think more highly of the person. If it eventually gets around to the person that you complimented them, they will likely feel appreciation for you. This will also likely cause people to trust you more. They will see that you don't trash talk people behind their backs. You actually build them up. They may feel more comfortable confiding things in you because they see the way you talk about others when they're not around. You definitely want to avoid gossip or divulging secrets, but if you can find a way to share something positive about a person with others, this is a great form of complimenting people.

There is one final thing related to compliments that I would be foolish to skip over, and that is encouragement. Encouragement can be a secret superpower. Giving encouragement is similar to giving compliments, but with some slight differences. Encouragement literally means "to give courage." It is about lifting people up and helping them to see their potential and their value. Sometimes it is given even though a person has made a mistake. Here the encouragement might be to not give up. Sometimes it is given when a person has created something beautiful in order to give them the courage to do it again. Sometimes encouragement is given when a person is facing a tough obstacle and needs a little help in order to face that obstacle. Encouragement is incredibly powerful.

Think of a time when you received encouragement from someone. It could be a coach, a parent, or a friend. How did it make you feel? Now imagine being able to give that same feeling to others. Guess what? You already possess that ability, and you possess it in an unlimited quantity! You can never run out! That is why I say encouragement is like a secret superpower. It is something that builds others up and you can give it out any time, in any amount. People will often remember you dearly for the encouragement you give them. It's almost never going to be received poorly. And like complimenting people, the more you make encouragement a habit, the more you will see the good in people because you will be conditioning yourself to look for it. You will start seeing people for their value and recognizing the potential they have inside, which is one of the main points of this book. It is going back to that core idea that everyone is a unique and valuable person made in the image of God. Learning to become an encouraging person is one of the best things you can do for yourself and for the world. As you see the value and potential in others, you will also see the value and potential in yourself. There are seriously so many benefits to encouraging others that I just can't emphasize it enough. It's so easy and so powerful. Start encouraging today!

CHAPTER 34

ACTIVE LISTENING

Listening is a great skill to have that will make you more likable, and help you to connect with people on a deeper level. Think of conversations from your own life. Can you think of examples where you could sense a person was there, but not really listening to you? How does that feel? Can you think of examples where someone was totally engaged, listening intently? How does that feel?

We like it when people listen to us. It shows us that the other person values what we have to say. It shows us that they don't think they are better than us. We feel understood. We feel connected. When someone is distracted, it feels totally different. Even if the person is engaged in the conversation, they might not be listening, and we can sense that too. If you have ever caught yourself trying to think of what to say next and spacing out on what the other person is actually saying, this is what I'm talking about. Listening is how we actually connect with people. There is a huge benefit to this.

When developing social skills, many people want to know the so called "magic words." How do I craft the perfect lines? What is the script? That way of thinking is incredibly superficial. Like I said before, it's not about what is said, but rather the connection that is happening between people. In any given conversation, you could let the other person do almost all the talking, and if you are intently listening, they will feel like they have known you for ages. If you tell the greatest story about yourself using the perfect lines, but don't listen to the other person, they might not feel like they know you at all. Did you catch what I just said? You could say almost nothing and connect more deeply with someone than by speaking the most clever, absolute best lines ever imagined! If you have a lot of confidence and want to test this, go up to people and don't say anything, but listen intently and try to convey something using only your body. Shockingly, you may find that you are actually able to connect with others without even saying a single word! That's how powerful listening is.

So what are some practical ways to do this? A lot of the social skills I mentioned previously will be helpful. First, make eye contact. Eye contact gets you zoned in on the other person. Next, you can try a form of mirroring. After the other person finishes saying whatever they have to say, repeat back to them a summary of what they said in your own words. This will force you to listen, in order to know what the other person said, and it will signal to them that you were listening. It will also prevent any misunderstandings. You are giving the other person the opportunity to correct you if you didn't interpret what they said correctly. It's totally fine if that happens. It's much better than getting deeper into the conversation and realizing you were not at all on the same page. The other person will recognize that you were engaged, and now you have the opportunity to clarify the communication between yourselves.

Another technique to help you become a better listener is to ask good questions. Open-ended questions are best. You will want to avoid anything that allows for simple yes or no answers. "Why" questions are great. When someone makes a statement about something, simply ask them why they believe what they do or did what they did. The more personal and relevant to the conversation, the better the questions will be.

Another tip for listening that might seem counterintuitive or uncomfortable at times is to let silence linger. When there is silence, don't immediately try to fill it with something. Get comfortable with letting it sit for a minute. Often the other person will start talking in order to fill the silence. Let there be pauses and spaces for reflection. Sometimes silence simply allows you both to process the information you just talked about. It's ok if nothing is being said. If you are ok with it, the other person will likely be ok with it. If you are always trying to fill the space, it's hard to listen. Your mind will be thinking of what to say next, rather than focusing on what is actually happening in the present moment. Listening is about being present with another person, and that's why it's so powerful for building connections. Learn to listen.

CHAPTER 35

SHARED EXPERIENCE

There are multiple ways a person becomes comfortable with another person, but the biggest one is through shared experience. The more experiences you share with another person, the more comfortable you become with them.

Think of a sports team. Initially, there is a random group of people who show up, most of them not knowing each other at all. At the beginning of forming the team, there is probably going to be a lot of tension and distrust. Some of the people might not even like each other. The season commences and the team starts to practice together. They all do the same workouts and drills. Slowly, the individual members of the team begin to feel more comfortable with each other. They learn each other's strengths and weaknesses. They understand how to better communicate with each other. As the season continues, they might start traveling to away games together, eating meals together, and winning or losing games together. All of these shared experiences take a group that was initially formed from a bunch of individuals and make them into a collective team. By the end of the season, the team is extremely comfortable with each other.

Another example of this phenomenon is easily visible in men who go to war together. The military is an organization that definitely understands how powerful shared experience is. This is one of the reasons why they shave everyone's head at bootcamp, and punish an entire group with pushups for the failings of one person. The shared experience bonds the group together. Actual combat takes things to another level completely. Men who go to war together seem to develop a brotherly bond that is impossible to break. It's because they have an extremely deep level of shared experience.

Shared experience is also why seeing someone repeatedly in class or at work can help you to feel comfortable with them. It's much easier to talk to someone you have seen at the same place 5 or 6 times than it is to talk to a total stranger. But what do we do if it's not possible to see someone 5 or 6 times? Well, if we know that shared experience creates comfort, we can leverage this to create comfort with people quickly, even if they are strangers. What do I mean? Shared experiences can be created through difficult physical challenges that you undergo with someone or seeing someone in the same location multiple times, but they can also be created through things like conversational threads or feeling different emotions. What I mean is that simply talking about a bunch of different subjects can have a similar effect to actually doing a bunch of activities together. Feeling multiple emotions can create the same bonds as seeing someone multiple times. The point I am trying to make is that if you want to build comfort with someone quickly, talk about multiple different topics or do things that will make for a bunch of different emotional responses.

Some people might think you have to go super deep on some heavy personal subject in order to get comfortable with someone. This is a myth. Creating the opportunity to have multiple shared experiences is actually how you develop comfort with people. Instead of staying in the same spot all night, take your friends to see multiple different sights and do multiple different activities. The greater the amount of shared experiences you can create, the more comfortable people will be with you.

CHAPTER 36

TALKING TO STRANGERS

Now that you've learned a bunch of different social skills, it's time to put them into practice. It's time to start approaching strangers. You may have already begun doing this, but in this section I want to specifically go through some strategies you can use when approaching strangers. This is by no means going to be an exhaustive list. There are many different situations, personality types, and viable ways of going about it. You might need to try multiple techniques before landing on something that works for you. Some things may feel awkward. Others won't fit your personality type. It's also unlikely that you will implement anything perfectly the first time trying it. Regardless of what strategies you employ, approaching strangers is probably going to feel unnatural at first. Like anything, it takes practice and experience. The biggest thing is that you get out there and start trying. The more people you talk to, the easier it will get.

As you begin, there are a couple of considerations you should keep in mind. First, a person's reaction will often reflect the energy you come in with. If you seem anxious and uncomfortable, the person you are approaching may express discomfort. If you come in with high energy and total confidence, the person may react with enthusiasm and energy themselves. Even if someone doesn't immediately mirror your attitude, they will at least be able to sense what you are feeling.

The second consideration is a caveat to the first. Though a person will probably react to you in some sense, it's also good to remember that their reaction isn't always a reflection of something *you* did. Often what happens in an interaction with a stranger has nothing to do with you. Perhaps the person just got off the phone after getting a call from their boss telling them they were fired. Perhaps they only got two hours of sleep the night before. There are a number of circumstances that you have zero control over, so don't take anything personally. Yes, starting a conversation from a place of comfort and confidence will increase the chances that it will go well. No, it will not guarantee the person you are approaching will even respond to you. There are just too many variables to take anything personally. Try to improve your approach, but also try to look at every interaction as a win, even if it ends in rejection. Being comfortable with rejection will actually improve your confidence anyways.

So, how does one approach a stranger and strike up a conversation? Like I said earlier, there are a plethora of things you could do. I will give you a few to try out, which should be plenty to get you started. Try not to make it too complicated. Performing some intricate routine with lines and movements is going to keep you in your head and cause the interaction to feel unnatural. Stay loose. Stay present in the moment. Don't worry about what you're going to say three questions down the road. Slow down. Listen to the other person.

When you first approach a person, you should try to be friendly, but also not over-the-top enthusiastic. You want to approach in a way that makes them feel comfortable. If you make a bee line and stop directly in front of someone, it might feel confrontational. If you come up from behind and grab their shoulder, it might startle them. If you can, it's good to try and get the person's attention a little before you get to them. You could make eye contact or make a subtle hand gesture showing that you want them to stop. Another good method is to come up alongside a person. When you do this it immediately establishes a cooperative tone to the interaction, which should inspire comfort. You can smile, say hello, and perhaps ask a question. A generic, "How's it going?" will work fine, but it's even better if you can make it more specific to the person or the situation. Before you even approach, you could try to make some observations. What is the person wearing? Are they doing anything interesting? Is there something interesting going on around you? Then formulate a question based on those observations. "What book are you reading?" "Where did you get that jacket? I really like it." These kinds of questions will help you stay in the moment.

Another strategy that works really well to engage

strangers is something called a cold read. This is when you make a statement about the person without knowing anything about them except what you can gather from external observations. You are basically trying to make an educated guess about them. For example, if I see someone in a coffee shop who is dressed like a lot of the other people there, I might go up to them and say, "You look like you're a regular here." This almost always gets a positive response. If you get the cold read right, the person will feel like you already know them. If you get it wrong, it often leads to an interesting follow up. For the coffee shop example, the person might respond with something like, "No, I'm actually not even from this country. I'm just visiting on holiday." This gives you the opportunity to get into a deeper conversation about whatever it is the person responds with.

This leads me to another consideration when approaching strangers. You might have to be the one who keeps the conversation going at first. Since you are the one initiating, this will be your responsibility until the other person commits to interacting with you. Often strangers aren't prepared to have someone approach them out of the blue and start talking to them. They may seem closed off at first. They don't know who you are. They don't know what you want. If you keep the conversation going, and show them that you aren't a weirdo or a salesman, they will often open up and engage. Don't harass anyone if they clearly don't want to talk to you, but if they simply seem a little closed off, just realize you might have to persist in keeping the conversation going until a higher level of comfort is established.

Once you're in a conversation, you can begin to use any of the skills we've covered so far. Often, if you get this far, you won't even be thinking about what you're doing anyways because the conversation will feel natural. If you like the person, you may decide that you want to try to stay in contact with them. If that's the case, a great way to do this is to try and find something you could do together. For example, if you discover that you both like country music, you could say something like, "Hey, I know this place that has great live country music. We should catch a show together sometime." Many people feel uncomfortable giving their contact info to strangers, but this method makes it easy because you are providing a reason for it. It also gives the person something to look forward to doing with you once you follow up with them. You could also do something similar by asking for advice if you learn the person has expertise in a field you're interested in. "Wow, that's really interesting. I would love to learn more about photography. Would you mind if I got your contact info and asked you some questions about it sometime?" The possibilities are almost endless.

If you are feeling really spontaneous, you could even invite the person to do something with you on the spot. This takes a lot more courage and confidence to pull off, but it can be a great way to start a friendship. "Hey, if you're free right now, we should go grab lunch at this awesome restaurant I know of." This is a bold ask, so don't be surprised if the other person is a little hesitant. Stay persistent, but also let them know it's totally fine if they choose not to. If they say no you could respond with something like, "No problem. Would you mind if I get your contact info, and we can try something in the future with a little more planning?" Just like any other interaction, they might say yes or they might say no. If the person does agree to do something with you on the spot, you will likely have an awesome experience to remember.

As you probably can see, all of this stuff is highly situational. There were a lot of "if, then" statements as I was trying to explain how to interact with strangers. Again, that is why doing it and getting experience is so important. The only way you are going to be able to learn what to do in any given situation is by trying it yourself and getting a feel for what works and what doesn't. Now, you should at least have a few ideas to try out. Being able to approach strangers is a skill that is difficult for a lot of people, but can be extremely rewarding. You will learn a ton and have the potential to massively expand your social network. It can lead to relationships with people you would have never otherwise encountered, and can even give you access to social circles that could totally change your life. It takes a lot of hard work, exposure to rejection, and time, but it's well worth the effort.

CHAPTER 37

ENERGY

A concept that we've touched on a few times now is that the way you make people feel is more important than the words you say. Again, I'm not talking about truthfulness in speech. That is always super important. What I mean is that a lot of people want to know the perfect script to make a social interaction go well, but it's probably 10% what you say and 90% how you say it that matters, and how you say things can't be faked. It's not like I can give you some lines, teach you how to say them, and then you can go in and do the perfect thing to make people like you. That isn't how it works. Referring to what I've hammered on so much throughout this book, you have to be speaking from a place of inner confidence. That is the most important thing. The energy you give off is what's going to either help people connect with you or push them away. And by energy, I don't mean some esoteric substance that flows through you like the force. I simply mean that the way you carry yourself and what you believe about yourself are things other human beings pick up on intuitively. If a dog or a horse can sense how you're feeling, how much more another human.

Have you ever met a person who acted really nice, but inside you just felt like something was off about them? That's because their actions weren't congruent with their inner beliefs, and you were able to sense that. People often just know when someone is being fake, so having the right lines and actions is never going to work if you haven't developed an attractive energy. I could give a perfectly crafted line to one of the people who just want to know what to say, and it wouldn't even help them. They wouldn't be able to say it in a way that's attractive. They might make a bunch of excuses to not use it at all, such as why the line isn't good enough, that they need to be prepared for a follow-up, or that it would work for someone else but not them. Even if they say the line and get a positive response, what happens after that? Until they work on their inner confidence and become at peace with themselves, there isn't a line in the world that will accomplish the results they're looking for. They may be able to squeak out a couple of positive interactions with people, but they will never be the type of person who feels comfortable in any situation, leads others, and has an amazing social life. You have to be changed at a core level in order to do that. You need to change your thought patterns, your habits, and all the little things that hold you back. Once you've developed inner confidence, then you will naturally start saying great things. You could learn lines at that point, but it wouldn't matter. You will already feel good about yourself no matter what you say, and people will be attracted to that.

Another way to understand energy is simply to start noticing how you feel. If you enter a new environment and feel anxious, others will probably see you as anxious. If you enter a new environment and feel confident, others will probably see you as confident. There might not be anything objectively different between an anxious person entering a room and someone who is confident entering the same room at the same time. They both might perform the exact same actions. Yet people would label the anxious person as anxious and the confident person as confident. So it's good to pay attention to how you're feeling. One trick that you can use if you are out and feel anxious, sad, or depressed is to allow yourself to suck. I've mentioned this before, but I'll describe it again. Simply accept that you feel crappy, go find a spot to sit or stand, and just let yourself totally suck for a couple minutes. Don't talk to anyone. Don't try to think of what you should say. Don't imagine what it would be like if you were super cool or famous. Simply allow yourself to suck, without putting any pressure on yourself. Look at yourself as the absolute champion of being boring. Often, after a minute or two of this, you will realize that nothing bad is happening to you. Everyone in the room isn't pointing and laughing. Most people probably don't even notice you. You will realize you're ok. This can relieve the pressure of having to perform and will hopefully relieve some of your anxiety as well. From there, try to engage with people coming from this newfound place of feeling ok. You will likely still have to push yourself outside of your comfort zone if you want to have good interactions, but hopefully the anxiety won't be overwhelming.

Again, if you have done the work and accepted that you are a unique unrepeatable person with infinite value and that God loves you, and you have developed inner confidence, socializing will not be an issue. You will feel comfortable in any situation because you understand that your value doesn't come from anything external. It is inherent based on you being made in the image and likeness of God. When this belief becomes grounded within you, your confidence will be unshakeable. You could enter a situation where people reject you using the most hostile demeaning words you can imagine, and it won't shake you.

That's why I've hammered so much on that message, especially before jumping into the social skills portion of this book. It's by far the most powerful thing you can do for your social life. I hope that the social skills I've outlined will help, but I want to end this section with repeating that relationships are more about what you believe than what you do. You have to become the person you would want to be in a relationship with. You have to change on the inside if you ever want real success.

CHAPTER 38

SOCIAL SKILLS CONCLUSION

So we just covered a lot of practical skills you can use in your social interactions. This is not an exhaustive list, and I have only scratched the surface on each of these topics. You could go much deeper on any one of them, and if you desire, you could even try to master some of them. Social skills are always going to be useful in life, so the more you practice and learn this stuff, the better off you are going to be.

For our intents and purposes, you now have plenty of techniques to try. I also want to remind you that social skills begin with inner confidence. You might be sick of hearing me say it at this point, but that stuff is much more important than any of these practical skills, as much as they are good to know. There will likely be this back-and-forth process of growing in confidence and getting better at the technical skills. The hope is that you will enter a cycle between the two that propels you upward in your ability to socialize and develop relationships. As you grow in confidence, the social skills should begin to come more naturally. At the same time, if you intentionally practice the social skills, you will get better at interacting with people, which will help you to continue growing in confidence.

Also keep in mind that you don't need to achieve perfection. Go easy on yourself and try to avoid beating yourself up. These are simply tools to help you grow. You are human. Most people are going to understand it if you seem a little awkward from time to time. They will appreciate that you are trying. You can even outright tell people you are trying to improve your social skills. It will take some of the pressure off, and other people will likely see it as a good quality in you. People like to be around others who are trying to improve themselves. They will probably appreciate the honesty, and they might even help and encourage you. The biggest thing is to be authentic. Sure, there will likely be some level of rigidity as you try to incorporate new skills for the first time. That's ok. If you keep at them, they will eventually become more natural. Even if the behaviors themselves feel robotic, the things they express should be authentic. For example, as you are trying to learn to compliment people, look for things you ACTUALLY like about them. Don't just say something to say something. Be genuine. In itself, this is a very attractive trait.

As you get better at the practical skills, it should actually become easier to be more authentic because you will be getting better at expressing yourself in different ways. The words you speak, the way you look at people, and the way you move your body are all different ways to communicate something. There might be a thought you have that words won't express, but maybe a gentle touch will. If you've practiced the skill of using touch, you'd be able to communicate those inexpressible thoughts much more authentically. So develop the inner confidence through the things mentioned in the first part of this book, and simultaneously start to practice the practical skills laid out here. Together this will be an explosive combination that will help your social life blow up...in a good way. Don't worry about getting it perfect. Just move forward and keep growing. Eventually you will look back and realize how tremendously you have grown.

CHAPTER 39

PITFALLS

So far we've covered a lot of ground. You should now have a good understanding of why relationships are important, what good ones look like, some ideas about how to become more confident, and lots of practical tools to improve your social skills. Still, there is one more important topic I want to cover. All the things I've brought up so far are ways to positively impact your relationships, but there are things that could negatively affect your relationships as well. I touched on this stuff a little bit at the beginning of the book, but I want to go deeper on some of these ideas now.

Some of these things are ideas our culture presents us. Others are behaviors you will want to avoid because they will end up sabotaging your relationships, kind of like antisocial skills, if you will. Some of these things are controversial. I hope that as you read through this section, my explanations about how these things affect us and why that's important will give you a better understanding of what's true and how you can live in a more virtuous way. You already know what will help you, but now you are going to learn what to avoid. It's important to do both.

Imagine someone is trying to get in shape and they take up a vigorous exercise routine, but eat donuts and guzzle soda all day. Beginning to exercise would be great, but their diet would undermine any positives they would have gained from it. In order to become fit, the person would have to incorporate the positives of exercise while simultaneously cutting out the negatives of junk food. In the following section, I'm going to show you what the junk food is. Some of it will probably seem obvious, but some of it is going to challenge you. It can be difficult to cut donuts from your diet, and it can be difficult to stop negative social behaviors. Try to read this portion of the book with an open mind, and try not to reject anything without hearing me out first. Once you get a full understanding, then you can do whatever you want.

The world has put many people in a daze. We are told things that make us dumbed down and weak. One of the reasons there is so much mental illness today is that our intuitive understanding of things doesn't match up with our perception of the world as it has been given to us. More simply, our beliefs don't match what we experience. When these incongruencies exist, it causes distress. Deep down we know the world is supposed to be one way, but we experience something else.

Many of the things we've been told about the world and how to interact with it are lies, and we sense that something else must be true. If we have not yet embraced this truth, we feel a tension between what we feel and what we experience.

In order to become totally free, we have to examine our thoughts and beliefs, confront the lies, and replace them with the truth. If we do this, then our identity will begin to match reality and we will experience peace and freedom. This sounds simple, and in a way it is, but it can also be quite difficult. For one, we tend to cling to the lies we believe because they are comfortable. Breaking them down means stepping into the unknown, which can be uncomfortable and even frightening. If you have believed something most of your life, and that belief has authored your mode of existence in the world, then changing it can feel like stripping yourself of existence itself. Yet, if that belief is a lie, then it's actually impeding you from an even greater form of existence. It's impeding you from freedom. Therefore, it's necessary to remove false beliefs so that you can truly start to live.

At the same time, you also have to be careful. Not everything you've ever been told is a lie. There are probably many things you believe that are true. There is nothing wrong with questioning those things. If an idea is true it should be able to stand up to scrutiny. However, there is always the inherent risk of throwing out the baby with the bathwater. There has to be at least some solid ground for you to stand on. If you have absolutely no idea what is true, then you will feel like you are lost. You will begin questioning reality. Sometimes things work the way they do simply because they give us a framework for how to operate in the world. There might be other ways to do things, but society has accepted a particular way simply because a choice needed to be made. This doesn't mean that whatever that choice was is false simply because other ways of doing things exist. It's important to be careful not to go around dismantling everything in sight. It will take some time to recognize the difference between what is an outright lie and what is just there because it was pragmatic. While you learn, it's a good idea to figure out what you know to be objectively true as a way to ground yourself in reality. That is the one caveat I would give as we begin to look at how this process works.

We've already talked about how replacing lies works on an individual level. Identify the lie. Identify what caused the lie. Replace it with the truth. The same process that works for lies you believe due to things that happened in your personal life is similar to the process that happens when addressing societal lies. Let's look at an example.

One societal lie you might believe is that uniformity is the same as unity. It's the lie that if you look and act like everyone else, you are united with them, and until everyone looks and acts the same, there is no unity. This is a lie and needs to be replaced with the truth that unity comes through love and does not depend on everyone being the exact same. It is actually our individual differences that complement each other and draw us closer together in unity. Think of a husband and wife. It's the very presence of both masculine and feminine that unite them together. Or think of a football team. Not everyone can be the quarterback. There needs to be a variety of skill sets in order for the team to perform well. When you have those different skill sets, then there can be unity. Though oftentimes uniformity can be one characteristic of unity, they are not the exact same thing. Yet, many people in modern society would have you believe that unity and uniformity are the exact same. The problem is, in order to fit into this box that you are presented with, you would have to repress some aspect of yourself, which could manifest in mental distress or other problems. It is only through rejecting the lie that uniformity equals unity and accepting the truth that people who are different can also be united that you will find freedom in that particular belief.

Again, you still have to be careful. You could go too far the other way and end up with anarchy. Unity also doesn't require things to be completely different in every regard. There will usually still have to be commonalities in whatever you are trying to unite. When it comes to people, it could be shared goals, beliefs, locations, or other characteristics. If you try to be entirely different, that won't work either. The ideal is somewhere in the middle, which is how it works with a lot of things.

When it comes to societal lies, these can be hard to spot because so many people believe them and go along living in accordance with them. The biggest things you can do to help spot these lies are to develop some critical thinking skills and familiarize yourself with the truth. Whenever someone suggests you do something that seems suspicious, question what their motivation is for getting you to do that thing. Ask lots of questions, and never do something just because it's popular. Form your mind with things you know to be true. When FBI agents are taught how to look for counterfeit currency, they spend most of their time examining the real thing. They get to know a real dollar so well that it is easy to spot a fake one. In the same way, if you can form your mind in the truth, you will be able to easily spot the lies.

Read the Bible. Read books that have stood up over time. Try to see if there are other perspectives you haven't considered. Find friends who are wise. Learning to spot the lies of society is a process that will take time, but it's worth it.

Once you begin to see the lies, do your best to act in a way that is truthful and never give in to them. This will be painful at times, at least in the short term. You may find that people attack you for it, or that you feel isolated. You may lose friends or career opportunities. You may even be persecuted and mocked. When people have bought into a lie, it is a challenge to their own existence when you live in the truth. At least that is how they will likely perceive it. Realize that you will never please everyone. Accept that you are going to face resistance, and embrace it to the best of your abilities. The reward is a soul that is free and at peace. With that, let me jump into some of the pitfalls of society.

CHAPTER 40

PORNOGRAPHY

The first issue I'm going to tackle is pornography, simply because it's so prevalent and so harmful. Pornography is plaguing millions of young men and women at this very moment. It is probably one of the largest industries in existence, and it's also one of the most dangerous and destructive. It may be the single most harmful thing for relationships in our time. Some people might think watching porn is something people do in private and that it doesn't really affect anyone, but that couldn't be further from the truth. It hurts the person using it, it hurts families, and it hurts those who are producing it. Pornography is not only wrong from a moral standpoint, it also causes innumerable problems on a biological and societal scale. There is scarcely anything more addictive a person can engage with.[15] It literally rewards one of our most primal instincts with just the push of a button. On top of all that, it's usually produced and consumed in secret, making it extremely difficult to address or get help with. The only way it can be stopped is if the individual people consuming it make the effort to stop. That's why I'm writing about it here. Hopefully, someone will read this and realize they want to stop using pornography and find some useful help for avoiding it.

I'll start with my own story. The first time I was exposed to pornography was when I was 9 or 10 years old. It is one of the few things I remember vividly from that age. I was watching TV alone. We had cable, and there were certain channels we weren't supposed to get, but for some reason they came through at times. I was switching through channels on the remote when I came across one of these channels. There was a clear picture, but it looked inverted like it was x-ray vision or something. The even stranger part was that there were naked women on the screen. I was too young to be aroused by it, but it still intrigued me. Once I knew this channel existed, I tried to find any chance I could to watch it. Of course, this was when my parents weren't around. I inherently knew something about it was bad, and so I didn't tell anyone. I kept this TV channel a secret. The process of hiding myself had begun.

When I got a little bit older, I started finding new ways to look at porn. First it was magazines and DVDs. Then the internet came along and exploded the possibilities. I became totally addicted, and my addiction only grew as I got older. I continued keeping it a secret, spending hours a day watching other people have sex while isolating myself. Using it regularly was all I had known since I was merely a child, so I had no idea of the effects it was having on my life. The way I looked at relationships, the way I practiced secrecy, the way my time and energy were being drained, the massive depression and anxiety it caused, and all the images that were permanently imprinted into my memory are all things I can only see in hindsight. I wish someone would have warned me about the dangers of pornography. I might have received some vague warning of, "Don't look at it," but I never had anyone explain why it was bad. If I would have known what it was going to cost me, maybe I would have avoided it. That's why I'm sharing this now.

The temptations and access to pornography are greater than ever. Almost everyone has a personal device they can pull out of their pocket and look up porn on from virtually anywhere at any time. I want to share the knowledge I learned about pornography use, so you can avoid it and maybe even help others avoid it too. I'm convinced that it is one of the worst things plaguing our society.

The first thing I'll mention about pornography is the way it affects the human brain. Porn is extremely addictive on a neurological level. It is an incredibly potent stimulus that releases massive amounts of dopamine in the brain.[16] Dopamine is a neurotransmitter associated with motivation and reward. When there is a huge dopamine release like that, it makes a person feel amazing. However, that feeling is only temporary and it comes with diminishing returns. A stimulus as powerful as porn sets a threshold for dopamine release, causing the brain to need progressively stronger stimuli to release the same amount of dopamine in the future. Basically, by using pornography, you are inoculating yourself to feeling pleasure. Any stimulus that doesn't hit that dopamine threshold that was set by your pornography use is going to seem dull and boring. This is why people who use porn lose their ability to be aroused. They often require more and more extreme forms of pornography.

Porn use can also lead to depression or anxiety. You are literally training your brain to expect massive rewards for doing something as easy as clicking a mouse. Humans were not designed to get that amount of pleasure from such weak efforts. We were designed with an incredibly strong drive to procreate wired into our brains. We have a primal desire to promulgate the human species. That means that the part of our brain that is wired for sex rewards us with massive amounts of pleasure so that we will be motivated to make more babies, and we will push through massive obstacles to do it. The problem with pornography is that you trigger those pleasure rewards without any difficulty at all. You can view more naked men or women in one session on the internet than most humans saw in their entire lifetimes in past eras. You are rewiring your brain in such a way that it expects the most primal of rewards for zero effort. As I stated earlier, this can lead to anxiety, depression, and many other problems. If you have inoculated yourself against experiencing pleasure, it is easy to see how you might lose interest in life.

Another problem with porn is the negative effect it has on relationships. There are a few reasons for this. First, you are learning to see people as objects of use for your personal pleasure. When you watch porn, the people in it are nothing but tools for making you feel good. There isn't any personal connection or commitment required. You don't learn about who the people you're watching are. You don't care how they feel. They are literally only there for your use.

With internet porn, you can even choose what types of people you want to use. You can filter out people who don't have a body type that is attractive to you. You get to pick and choose any characteristics you like. All of those things condition you to only be attracted to perfection, at least what you perceive to be perfection. The problem is, that isn't how relationships in real life work. When you want to find a mate in real life, a porn user is going to have all these expectations that are impossible to fulfill. They are going to expect sex at the snap of a finger. They are going to expect a perfect body type. They aren't going to expect rejection when it inevitably comes. The person they desire doesn't exist, and so they will be frustrated. That's just one effect porn will have on your relationships.

Another is that porn users often train themselves to be secretive. Pornography is something viewed behind closed doors and in private. Most people feel a sense of shame around it, even if they don't consider it wrong. They are embarrassed about other people seeing them or even knowing what they do. Yet, they have no problem watching others have sex, many of whom are being abused and exploited. When you habitually hide something like this, you start to build walls around yourself. You become unable to be vulnerable. If you have read pretty much any other part of this book, you know that vulnerability is incredibly important for building relationships. This conditioned secrecy that happens with porn addiction will eventually render you unable to be vulnerable or authentic. Combine the massive dopamine hits with conditioning yourself to be secretive, building walls against vulnerability, and you have a recipe for apathy. Trust me. Apathy is not going to help you with anything in life. And those aren't even the only ways your relationships could be affected!

Related to the secrecy problem is the temptation to lie about porn use. If you are dating someone or are married, the last thing you want to do is destroy trust. Yet most people aren't going to want their mates to watch other people have sex. It might make them jealous or make them feel like they aren't good enough for you, and in reality, you might actually start losing attraction for them as well. The only way to continue using porn while being able to avoid those issues is by lying. But lying will ruin your relationship. Eventually what is done in darkness will be brought to light, and it will lead to a reckoning you probably don't want to have. The best thing to do for your relationships is to avoid pornography at all costs. The quick temporary pleasure hits you get are miniscule gains for such a high cost.

Next, I will briefly talk about the moral problems of pornography. One of God's Commandments is "You shall not commit adultery." (Exodus 20:14) During the earthly life of Jesus, He took it a step further, "You have heard that it was said, 'You shall not commit adultery.' But I say to you that everyone who looks at a woman with lustful intent has already committed adultery with her in his heart." (Matthew 5:27-28) What is pornography but looking at people with lust?

As I stated earlier, pornography turns people into objects of use for sexual gratification. This is morally wrong. It goes against God's Commandments and it hurts people. Society may recognize the evils of sex trafficking, but it does not want to address the problem of pornography, which is one of the root causes of sex trafficking. When there is such a high demand for porn, people will find ways to produce it, even if it means extreme abuse and exploitation. Even the people who voluntarily get into it often end up with all kinds of problems. They may start to put all their worth in their bodies or get addicted to drugs. They might have kids without a father or mother to help raise them. As soon as these porn stars aren't desirable anymore they are kicked to the curb with no one to help them. With the advent of things like OnlyFans creating smaller barriers to entry, the average person can get involved in pornography and make easy money without realizing the degradation that is happening to them.

Imagine an industry that makes an incredible amount of money and has more viewership than Amazon, Netflix, and Twitter combined, yet there isn't any mention of it at all in the public square.[17] That should tell you that there is something wicked going on here. It reveals that people intuitively know pornography is shameful. It is literally the largest media industry in the world and you never hear about it. That's insane! Pornography is a dark and disturbing industry.

Hopefully, by now you are convinced that pornography should be avoided at all costs, but what can you do if you or someone you know is already addicted? First, know that it is possible to be free from pornography addiction. I was highly addicted for around 15 years, and yet I have been free for around 7 years at the time of writing this. It is possible to stop.

First, I would suggest really calculating the cost of using pornography. Write down all the things you are losing when you use porn, and be brutally honest about it. I'll give you a few examples to get you started. You are losing time and energy. You are missing out on healthy relationships and true love. You are losing your own dignity. You are ruining your family. You are losing the enjoyment of many positive experiences due to the rewiring of your brain. You are missing career opportunities due to lack of motivation. That is just the tip of the iceberg. The list could go on. However, there is one cost that is greater than all the rest combined. Willfully viewing pornography puts your eternal soul in danger. You could actually be risking eternal life in the Kingdom of God by willfully using pornography. That is one cost that isn't even close to worth the risk.

Next, I want you to list the potential benefits to quitting. Here are some more examples. Your brain will reset and work normally again. You will gain time and energy you can put towards other things. You will be able to be more authentic and confident. You will be able to experience true love. You will have time to spend with your family. Write down whatever it is that matters most to you.

When you understand the cost of using pornography and

the potential benefits of quitting, that will be your motivation. That will be your why. You could even tape a list of these things next to your computer or wherever you might be most tempted to use pornography, so that you remember why you are quitting. Use a visual such as a picture of your kids if you have to. Do whatever it takes!

Another thing I would do is get a friend or some other accountability partner. You are going to be less likely to use porn if you know someone is going to ask you about it. An accountability partner will also give you someone to reach out to if you are struggling. Getting a professional counselor can help as well. If you do happen to use pornography as you begin this process of quitting, don't be too hard on yourself. Just resolve not to use it again as quickly as possible. Don't overcomplicate it. There are many tools available to quit and certain ones might work better or worse, depending on the person.

What you don't want to do is let the tools become an excuse to fail. What I mean is that sometimes people get it in their minds that they just don't have the right tool yet, or that they need more support, or that they need some perfect combination of things that doesn't actually exist. Once they find the golden remedy, *then* they will be able to quit. What they are actually doing is giving themselves excuses to keep using porn, while simultaneously making themselves feel like they are doing everything they can. Not only will this prevent you from being free, but it will make you feel discouraged because you will believe you are trying everything, yet continuing to fail. If that happens, it will make you want to give up altogether.

So much of this is about your mindset and what you believe. Avoid saying things like, "I'm struggling with this," or "I'm an addict." These things reinforce the mindset that you aren't actually free. In order to be totally free, you have to actually believe you are totally free. You have to convince yourself that you are a new person, and the old one no longer controls you. Watching porn is just something you don't do because that's not who you are. A great way to reinforce this shift in identity is through prayer. Ask God to help you, and then preach His promises to your heart. He will give you the strength to change. That's not to say you won't be tempted ever again. You certainly will be. But you need to develop the strength to say no to those temptations. Remember the cost and remember the rewards. Keeping your why in mind will give you the motivation to keep going.

CHAPTER 41

LIFE ISSUES

Most people would agree that human life is inherently valuable. However, there are some major disagreements about what that means in modern society. One of the current prominent issues at the time of writing this is abortion. Abortion is the voluntary ending of a human life inside his or her mother's womb. There are two main camps people fall into with this issue, and there are a variety of beliefs within each one. The first camp is the pro-life position, which posits that abortion is wrong, and the second is the pro-choice position, which posits that individual women should be able to choose whether or not to have an abortion. The population, at least in the United States, is divided pretty evenly between the pro-life and pro-choice positions. However, most people would at least say that they don't think abortion should be done after a certain point in a pregnancy. Where people consider that point to be tends to differ.[18]

I believe that if we can come to a clear understanding on a few key ideas, we would see that abortion is wrong in all circumstances. Some of you reading this might be totally abhorred by even considering that. You might believe abortion is a human right and so it feels like that is being challenged. Some of you might think that abortion is wrong, but that exceptions should be made for things like incest or rape. Others might be totally in agreement with me that abortion is wrong under all circumstances. Wherever you're at, try to at least hear me out. Like I said, we are covering some controversial ground in this section of the book. It is going to take an open mind to grapple with some of these ideas. Yet, I hope you will see that they are important enough to at least read about and consider.

There was a point in my life where I could have cared less about abortion. I thought it was simply a medical procedure that stopped a pregnancy. I had never looked into it that deeply and I didn't even consider what was really going on in an abortion. I was told pro-lifers were nuts and so I just figured whatever they believed was nonsense. I actually had an experience with abortion in the form of the morning after pill. After sleeping with a girl one night, I convinced her to get the morning after pill a couple days later. She wasn't on contraception because it messed up her body, and she informed me that the morning after pill would also mess her up. I told her she should get it anyways and that I would pay for half of it. It was a scumbag move that I still regret. The morning after pill might not seem that extreme, but it still feels strange knowing that I might have potentially had a child, especially because I don't know if I will be able to have children anymore due to my paraplegia.

Later, when I actually looked into what abortion was, I was shocked. It was so painfully obvious that I had been blind. Even after becoming a Christian, I didn't really have a strong sense that abortion was wrong, though I knew many Christians were pro-life. The thing that really changed my mind was learning what actually happens in abortion. That's it. Just learning the facts. Once I knew, there was no going back.

Again, you might be asking something like, "What does abortion have to do with relationships?" I would reply, "Everything." The reason I'm writing about abortion is that our views and mindsets about human life have a tremendous effect on our relationships. These views are fundamental to establishing a secure identity as unique human beings with inherent value. I've written about the importance of this throughout this book. In order to be successful in relationships, you have to be confident in your identity and understand your value as a human being. The way we see human life in general, in the womb or elsewhere, has a major impact on how we view ourselves as well. Let's take a look at abortion and hopefully you will see what I'm talking about.

First we have to establish when life begins. This is very important because if what we are talking about is not a human life, then it doesn't matter what we do and this conversation is basically irrelevant. However, if it is a human life, then it can be nothing other than murder because murder is the deliberate ending of a human life. Like I mentioned earlier, many people think that abortion is wrong at some point. Most people wouldn't condone ending the life of a perfectly healthy 8 month old who could be born at any moment, though there are some people who would even go that far in their support for abortion. That is on the extreme side of things though, at least for now.

So where should we draw the line? After there's a heartbeat? After the fetus can feel pain? After the second trimester? If we get into this kind of debate, it becomes arbitrary. This is the precise reason some people argue that the mother should be able to choose whether to get an abortion or not. They will say that it's impossible to figure out when life begins. But is that true? Do we not have any reasonable criteria for determining when life begins?

The field of biological science would argue otherwise. Any biologist will tell you that we actually can point to a specific time when life begins. That point is at fertilization. The moment the male sperm fertilizes the female egg, a new human life is formed, containing its own unique set of DNA. From then on, at every stage of pregnancy, the organism that is growing inside the womb of its mother is a unique human being. The only difference is the level of development. Just as an infant is different from a toddler, and a toddler is different from a teenager in their level of development, a 4 week old fetus is only different from a 4 month old fetus in his or her level of development. From the moment of fertilization he or she is always a unique human being.

Ask any woman who has had a miscarriage if there was a human life inside of her. Then ask her if the miscarriage was traumatic at all. From my experience, the women I've talked to who have had miscarriages grieve as if they've lost a child, because they have. Now imagine how traumatizing it would be if that woman found out that she was the cause of her miscarriage.

The rallying cry of, "My body, my choice," does not make sense. When it comes to pregnancy, we are not talking about one body, but two. We should certainly have a right to agency over our own bodies, and I would not try to take that away from women or anyone else. The problem with abortion is that it does take that right away from a person, a person who is so powerless that they are unable to speak a word in defense of that right. The fact of the matter is that the whole of pregnancy involves two separate human lives, a mother and a child.

In this case, the choice over what happens to one's own body comes along with the choice to have sex, not after it. God has created us in such a way that when we engage in sex we are able to create new life, which is why we also experience intense pleasure from it. We have a built in reward system that drives us to make more babies and perpetuate the human race. Again, one of the reasons pornography is so dangerous is because it activates those reward systems with the click of a button. Pornography might be an extreme example of desiring to have pleasure without consequences, but the same attitude is often behind the desire for abortion to be legal, and also the desire to use contraception, which I will cover shortly. Basically, we want to receive the benefits without dealing with the consequences. This explains a lot of things in life. Some people want to lose weight without dieting or exercise. Others fall for get-rich-quick schemes. Some people even buy fake Louis Vuitton bags in order to feel like they are rich, without actually putting in the effort to get rich. This attitude is all over society, and it's sad.

Desiring the right to choose whether or not to have an abortion after engaging in sex would be similar to going to a car dealership, spending your money on a car, driving it off the lot, and then returning to the dealership 3 months later, saying that you actually didn't want the car, and then expecting a refund. The salesman would look at you like you're nuts. Everyone knows that once you hand over the money, the car has been sold. When humans engage in sex, babies are made. That is the natural consequence of that act. Trying to justify a choice later on is only the result of a selfish desire for pleasure and lack of self control.

This is where someone might bring up cases of rape and incest because women don't choose to have sex in those situations. Shouldn't someone have a choice about abortion if they find themselves pregnant after being raped and abused? First, I want to acknowledge that those are horrible experiences women have been forced into. No matter what actions follow, these women have been wounded and traumatized. I'm not writing this section flippantly. I care a lot about the well being and safety of women. The last thing I want is for any of them to end up in a situation like that, but the harsh reality is that some do. The reason I'm even writing about this is because we need to consider our responses to these situations and provide solutions that will be the most effective in terms of actually helping these women heal. Someone will say that's why we should place that decision in the hands of the woman who was just victimized. It makes sense, right? Only if you oversimplify things to the extreme. Have you considered that a woman who has just been traumatized by rape might not have the greatest judgment? Have you considered that she is probably only hearing one perspective and doesn't have sufficient information available to her to make a good decision? Have you considered the research on what actually provides the best outcomes in terms of healing and happiness for victims of rape? If it turned out that the vast majority of women who conceived a child through rape or incest reported being happier when they chose to keep their child, would you tell them that?[19]

Abortion isn't going to solve anything. For one, the child isn't the problem, the crime that was committed is. Let's say someone running from the cops hit another person's child with a stolen car, and the child now has many medical bills that the parents can't afford. Would you walk up to the mother of that child and tell her, in her distress, that the best option is for her to hire someone to kill her child since the child's medical bills will be a burden and she will always be reminded of the man who hit her child due to some disfigurement that occurred? That would be insane! We would never say that the way to solve that problem is to kill the child. It would be a horrible injustice that only causes more trauma. We would rightly see the child as an innocent victim of a horrible crime, not the problem. We would demand justice for the driver, not the child. So why would we encourage abortion for someone who has conceived a child in rape or incest? Why should the innocent child pay for the crime of the abuser? It would only cause more trauma and perpetuate the violence that was done to the victim. It would actually turn the victim into the perpetrator, which could easily end up being the most traumatizing part of all. Abortion is not going to solve anything.

A better solution would be to provide total support for the victim, make sure she is taken care of, and encourage her as a mother. If looked at with the right perspective, the child could give tremendous meaning to the suffering of the victim, and meaning is one of the most important ingredients of healing from that kind of trauma.[20] The child could be a huge blessing that came out of a horrible situation. It's all about how we look at it, which brings me to the underlying issue I see in the debate on abortion.

Do we see life as a blessing or a burden? If we see human life as a blessing, we are going to value that life. We are going to do everything in our power to support that life. We wouldn't even dare try to eliminate it. On the other hand, if we see human life as a burden, we are going to act much differently. We are going to view people as disposable. Instead of having intrinsic value, the only value someone has becomes what they can contribute to society. Don't get me wrong, it is important to contribute to society, but that isn't where value is derived. In case you don't see why this would be a problem, let me give you some examples.

With this worldview, if someone is elderly and needs special care to stay alive, it is better to just let them die, or at least put them in a nursing home where they aren't a burden to us. If someone has a disability and needs help to achieve their goals, that becomes their own problem. And if someone gets pregnant and doesn't want the burden of raising a child, then they should get an abortion. Of course, my point is not that a child is a burden. Neither is an elderly person, and neither is a disabled person.

Sometimes we don't even realize the gift people with lesser abilities actually are. Perhaps the elderly person passes on wisdom you use later in life. Perhaps the disabled person shows you how to care for others. Perhaps the child encourages the mother when she is in a rough spot at work. We simply can't understand the interconnected web of our lives and how we affect each other. When we see life as a burden, we end up trying to destroy that web, sometimes destroying the very thing that was meant to help us.

Oftentimes this "life is a burden" mindset can even lead to our own self-destruction. What do I mean? If you see human life as a burden in general, you may even begin to see your own life as a burden specifically. If that happens it is likely going to lead to major depression, anxiety, and a potential host of other mental health issues. Perhaps that is one of the reasons suicide rates are so high at the time of writing this.[21] The world has been bombarding people with the idea that they are only valuable for their beauty, riches, skills, and youth. If someone believed they were missing one of those things, they could easily internalize that and believe they are worthless. The major idea I've been hammering on throughout this book is that you are a unique human being with dignity and value. Understanding that is foundational for developing confidence. When you believe the opposite, it causes doubt, fear, and dissatisfaction with life. That's why abortion is such an important issue. If we align ourselves to the side that says life is a burden, it will have massive negative consequences. If we see life as a blessing, we are going to cherish it and value it on all levels.

This is also part of the reason contraception is bad. Some of you might be thinking, "Wouldn't the use of contraception prevent the need for abortion?" This is tricky, so bear with me a bit. That is actually the argument that people used when they first pushed contraception decades ago.[22] They said that once contraception was introduced to society, abortion rates would plummet. That's actually the opposite of what happened. Abortion rates rose.[23] There could be a multitude of reasons for this, but I'm going to go back to mindset, because both contraception and abortion are the result of a similar mindset.

There is the mindset of wanting pleasure without consequence that I covered earlier, and there is the mindset that life is a burden, which are both present in the use of contraception. There may be other mindsets and beliefs involved, but these are the two main ones I've seen pushed, and they are the two most destructive. If people believe life is a burden, it follows that they would desire to have access to contraception and abortion. They are seeing human life as a problem. By pushing contraception, society is basically promoting the idea that the creation of human life is something that should be stopped. If that is what society tells us, perhaps you can see how that could cause many in society to start supporting abortion too. If there is no value for human life, why would abortion even be controversial? It isn't much of a leap to go from stopping life using contraception to stopping life through abortion.

Contraception also promotes the idea that sex and pleasure are to be valued above all else. "We should be able to have our pleasure without those pesky consequences!" This has led to all kinds of issues from promiscuity to the breakdown of families. It takes sex from being an amazing act of love involving a total gift of self, and turns it into a mundane act strictly used for pleasure. It actually makes people see each other as objects that are only there for pleasure. If you don't have to raise a child with someone, it doesn't matter what happens to them. The mindset behind contraception and abortion is incredibly insidious.

On top of that, contraception has been shown to have many negative side effects for women on a biological level. It messes with their hormones and can even do strange things like change their sense of smell. That might not seem like a big deal until you realize that smell is one of the ways humans are attracted to each other, and women who meet their mate while on contraception often lose attraction for them if they stop taking it later in the relationship. Women who are on contraception have also been shown to be attracted to more feminine men, which could disrupt the sexual dynamics of society for both women and men.[24]

The consequences of taking contraception can be devastating. It increases divorce rates, it contributes to sex trafficking, and it is a rejection of the very gift of life that God offers us.[25] Again, this is a book on relationships. Contraception and abortion are both horrible for relationships. They foster indifference towards human life and distrust in relationships. If you are looking for a strong marriage at some point in your life, contraception and abortion are two of the worst things you can introduce to that relationship. Life is not a burden. It is a wonderful gift. As a society, we need to start changing our perspective on these things, and it can start right now with you. Hopefully, by reading these sections of this book, your eyes will be opened to what's really going on and what's really at stake. And just like with pornography, willfully procuring an abortion puts your eternal soul at stake. God does not take the killing of innocent life lightly. If you have already participated in an abortion, I encourage you to repent and seek forgiveness. God is merciful when we confess our sins.

CHAPTER 42

SEXUALITY AND IDENTITY

I want to start this chapter by stating that my intention with what I am about to write is not to disparage anyone in any way. People who struggle with their identity or sexual attractions don't deserve to be insulted or belittled. The point of this chapter is to share the truth about these issues. That is the loving thing to do. Some people may think that I am singling out homosexuality and transgenderism here. Christians are often accused of making these things out to be the greatest sins a person could commit. I can see how someone might arrive at this conclusion, but it is mistaken. All sin is equally wicked. In the gospel of Luke, Jesus is talking to a crowd about some Galileans who died in a gruesome manner. He says, "Do you think that these Galileans were worse sinners than all the other Galileans, because they suffered in this way? No, I tell you; but unless you repent, you will all likewise perish." (Luke 13:2-3) A married man may have the desire to cheat on his wife with other women. That's a sexual desire that is just as disordered as homosexuality. Another man might have the desire to rob people and steal their stuff. Just because he has that desire doesn't make it right. The reason homosexuality and transgenderism need to be talked about specifically is due to the fact that they are celebrated in our culture. No one is throwing parades celebrating adultery. No one is inviting convicted felons into libraries to read kids stories about committing robbery. The *celebration* of homosexuality and transgenderism is the problem. It's causing confusion and chaos in society, so clear teaching about what these things really are is needed. I'm not trying to attack anyone. I don't hate anyone because of these things. This is about exposing lies and sharing the truth. It's about warning people of the great dangers of these ideologies.

In this book, I've stated over and over again how important being secure in your identity is. You have to be grounded in who you are if you want to become confident and have healthy relationships. The idea that a person can change their gender is totally contrary to this. Biology is clear. There are males and females. A few extremely rare exceptions can occur in people who are intersex and have a physical makeup that doesn't fit neatly into the male or female categories. However, those are biological abnormalities that can be clearly defined. The idea that someone was born in the wrong body is much different. It is a disorder of the mind, not the body. The solution then, has to be one for the mind, and not the body.

When people are told they are right in believing they are in the wrong kind of body and are encouraged to physically alter that body through surgery and hormone therapy, they are being misled. The right solution is to try to help them come to a place of acceptance in their mind, not their body. However, this becomes near impossible when it is not allowed to call the problem a disorder. If you can't define what is going on, you can't fix it.

Imagine if someone tried to claim that suicidal ideation was not a disorder. Imagine that you were told you had to affirm someone who is suicidal, and tell them to go through with it. That would rightly be called insane. Yet, this is exactly what is happening with transgender and homosexual ideologies being pushed in modern culture. It is especially destructive when children are the ones being indoctrinated with it.

Working as a cognitive trainer, I started to see these ideas being pushed on the kids I was working with. For example, I had a second grader who came to her training session and told me that she got to pick her pronouns earlier that day at school. There was another kid who I'm fairly confident was a boy who was being raised as a girl. These ideas are sowing confusion amongst children and it will lead to even greater dysfunction and suffering. Children need guidance and leadership. They need truthful answers about who they are so that they can learn to operate within the confines they've been given.

We all have limits, and the best way to operate is to accept those limits and do our best within them. There are lots of things we aren't able to choose in life. We can't choose the parents we have, the DNA we've been given, where we are born, or what period of history we are born in. If I believed I was born in the middle ages, that doesn't mean it's true, and trying to act like I was would only cause distress. We would rightly call that disordered thinking. So why are we unable to call transgenderism disordered? Why are children being given hormone blockers that will permanently alter their bodies when their brains are developing so rapidly that it is impossible for them to even have a concept of sexuality or gender? It's insanity, and that can be seen in the consequences.

For example, look at women's sports where biological males who identify as female have been allowed to compete. They dominate the competition. Look at the examples from female prisons, where biological males who identify as female were allowed to transfer in and ended up impregnating other inmates.[26]

This idea that someone can change their gender is causing massive destruction in our society. There are male humans and female humans, and we are born with the body that belongs to us. We can't change our chromosomal make-up. We can't change our bone structure. Any changes made to sex organs are only superficial. They don't provide any actual utility. We have to learn to accept the body we've been given. This is the only way to become truly confident and have successful healthy relationships.

It is a very similar situation with homosexuality. Though at least it doesn't involve permanent bodily mutilation, it is still a disorder of identity. Men and women were each created for a specific function and purpose. Sex is a complementary behavior that requires both a male and a female. Again, this is easily seen in the biological structures of men and women, as well as the results of sex. Sex is meant for the propagation of the human species. When a man and a woman come together in sex, they create children. A man and a man will never create children. A woman and a woman will never create children.

Homosexuality is a disorder of identity because it refuses to accept the sexual role that is normal for a man or a woman to have. Trying to normalize it doesn't actually make it normal, it makes it acceptable. But that is a terrible idea because a lie has to be used to accomplish that goal, the lie that homosexuality is normal. Look, I know this sounds controversial to many people. I sympathize with the people who have homosexual desires. I can't imagine what it would be like to feel that way. But when it comes to the point of teaching young children that homosexuality or transgenderism is normal, I have to draw a line. It is literally propagating disorder and confusion. It is causing immense suffering in the lives of those who are the most vulnerable.

I'm not advocating for anything crazy here. All I'm saying is that we should call these things what they are. That doesn't mean persecuting people with homosexual desires. It doesn't mean banishing anyone from society. Anyone struggling with a disorder deserves care and compassion. We should try to help them in any way possible, but that doesn't have to happen at the expense of truth or children's development. If a person has anorexia, we wouldn't cast them out of society or mistreat them, but we also wouldn't teach people that being anorexic is a good thing or that it should be embraced. We try to help them get out of the anorexia so they can live a happy and fulfilling life. Can we do the same with these issues?

CHAPTER 43

CASUAL VS COMMITTED

Around the end of middle school and beginning of highschool I began to experience this pressure to begin sexual exploration. Most of the other boys I knew, as well as myself, had already encountered pornography. This combined with raging pubescent hormones made for a very dangerous view of sexuality. Some boys started sexually experimenting with girls and they would report back to all the other boys what happened. Pretty soon it turned into this sort of contest to see who could gain the most sexual experience. The boys who started hooking up with girls were the ones who were celebrated and lifted up as leaders. In the mind of the group, the only possible reason you hadn't hooked up with a girl was that you were a loser. There was no talk of dignity or value. There was no talk of commitment. It was simply a game of who could rack up the most notches on their belt.

This game only intensified as I got older. There was so much pressure to have sex at my highschool that I can only think of two of the attractive girls I knew who made it through without losing their virginity, and I don't even know if those two for sure made it. I just never heard any guys brag about hooking up with them. I was always embarrassed to have those conversations with other guys, not because I thought they were repulsive, but because I hadn't lost my virginity yet. The mentality that hooking up with more girls made you more of a man really messed with my self-confidence. So I became laser focused on trying to do just that. I thought that if I started having more casual hookups, it would suddenly make me worthy of being called a man.

I hadn't lost my virginity yet when I started college, but it seemed like the perfect place to begin my conquest. There were no authority figures holding me accountable, and I was free to do whatever I wanted without consequence. Plus, I felt this urgent need to prove my manhood even more intensely. Even then, it took until my sophomore year to actually lose my virginity. I would like to look back and say that it was a magical experience, but it wasn't.

It started with me downing an entire bottle of Goldschlager, which caused me to blackout before I even left my dorm room. I woke up lying next to my date, my neck feeling incredibly sore. I then learned that I had gotten off a party bus when we got back to campus and started cussing out this guy on the wrestling team. He immediately ran over, dropped me to the ground, and started strangling me. My date ran up and socked him in the face. She may have very well saved my life. After she told me the story, we had sex. I think I was expecting some sudden moment of enlightenment or something, but it never happened. There were a few moments of pleasure and then I went back to feeling the same as I did before. I dated this girl for a short time and then broke her heart by getting with a different girl. I thought, maybe I just needed more experience. So, the quest to prove my manhood continued. Compared to a lot of other guys I knew, I was by no means a player, but I had my fair share of casual hookups after that. None of them led me to the fulfillment I was seeking.

Later in life I began to look back on my past and see missed opportunities. I saw all these potential hookups I could have had, and wished that I would have gone through with them. There was this twisted line of thinking that made me believe that I would be more fulfilled if I would have hooked up with more women. I still didn't feel like a man. Then it struck me. If I had hooked up with more women, they would still only be memories. That's what my life was filled with. Memories. Shadows. Vapors. No wonder I wasn't fulfilled. That's the thing no one ever tells you about casual sex. The pleasure lasts for a moment and then it's gone, leaving only calloused hearts and vague memories. In the big picture of life, it's worthless.

I could give you tons of reasons why casual sex is a bad idea. It decreases your ability to connect with people. It could lead to unplanned pregnancies or STDs. Even just the fact that it's not really that good is a reason not to do it. Plus, married couples statistically have way more sex than single people.

However, the thing that strikes me most about it at this stage in my life, is that by engaging in casual hookups, you are literally trading a solid lasting family for memories that are basically worthless. You can't wake up next to a memory. You can't drop a memory off at school and watch it develop into a strong young man or woman. Memories are only there to help us make better decisions in the present or for fantasizing over. They hold no tangible value. Having someone to share your life with is real. Having children is real. Marriage is the true path to having fulfilling relationships. It's built on vows. It's built on long term commitment. It's solid. The problem with casual hookups is that they're illusions. I thought that I would find fulfillment if I just hooked up with enough women, all the time neglecting the path that would have led me to start a family. It's like Esau trading his birthright for a bowl of lentils (Genesis 25). Thankfully, I'm young enough that I can still start that family, though I would have saved myself from a lot of trouble if I would have just realized all this from the beginning.

CHAPTER 44

COHABITATION AND DIVORCE

These next two things I will cover are quite related to each other and can be the consequences of other dysfunctional behaviors discussed earlier. I'll start with cohabitation. Cohabitation is when two people in a romantic relationship are living together without being married. This one can seem like it's not that big of a deal. Maybe the couple living together intends to get married. Maybe they are sleeping in separate beds. Maybe they want to test things out before they get married. The problem with cohabitation is that people living together are living like they are married without the commitment of marriage.

Marriage is an institution of trust. That means that it is based on commitment. When people cohabitate, their relationship is based on a "maybe" rather than an "I do."

There is no decisive choice about the other person. People who cohabitate often don't discuss how they are going to live together and what that will mean for the relationship. If there is sexual intimacy during the time of cohabitation, that only complicates things even more. We also know that couples who cohabitate before marriage tend to report less satisfying marriages and have higher rates of divorce.[27] It makes sense if you consider that there is no commitment while cohabitating. Rather than committing oneself to the other person, it's making a practice of leaving the door open for other opportunities. It is adopting the mindset of, "I'll stay with you unless something better comes along." Cohabitation reinforces the idea that relationships are interchangeable. This leads me into the next subject, divorce.

Divorce has become a major issue in the current generation. I am a child of divorce myself, and I've experienced how destructive it is from the child's perspective. I get that there are situations of serious abuse or danger that require separation, but what I'm talking about is the way marriage and divorce are looked at today. Marriage has lost the sense of commitment that it used to have. People look at it as a commitment that can be broken simply because they don't want it anymore. Things like prenuptial agreements, which are common nowadays, are a great illustration of this. If marriage is supposed to be founded on trust, a prenuptial agreement totally undermines that. It basically sets the expectation that at some point divorce is going to happen. I get that there are many people who have lost a lot in divorce. There are even people out there who marry someone rich intentionally, knowing that they will divorce them and take their money. This is a horrible reality of modern society. However, the solution is not to try to protect oneself by building walls against trust. If you want a marriage that will last there has to be vulnerability. There has to be risk. Prenuptial agreements communicate that you value material possessions more than the person you are marrying.

Because of the denigrated view of marriage that has infected our society, we have started to build walls, which don't allow for true connection and lifelong love. The reason marriage is so important is that it provides a safe place for the couple to bond sexually and for the raising of children. In order to develop properly, children require both a mother and a father. Children who are missing one of these tend to have much worse life outcomes on a variety of measures.

This is also why homosexual couples don't provide a proper environment for the raising of children. Having two moms or two dads doesn't provide the children with both masculine and feminine guidance. Children need the masculine protection and leadership of a father and the feminine nurturing care of a mother. Statistics show that children raised by homosexual couples also have worse life outcomes than children raised by both a mother and a father.[28] A proper view of marriage is one that is between one man and one woman, but let's return to the topic of divorce.

A problem children can face when their parents divorce is experiencing an unsafe environment. Children are unable to flourish and grow if they are living in fear. This can occur because the parents fight all the time, because one of the parents leaves, or a combination of different traumatic experiences. Children of divorce often struggle with their own relationships later in life. Sometimes they are afraid of intimacy because they think it will always end poorly. Sometimes they become controlling because things felt out of control during the divorce.

One thing I remember struggling with during my parents' divorce was feeling like I was all alone. I felt different than everybody else. In school my friends would talk about what they did with their families over the weekend, or someone would ask me a question about my family and I would instantly feel a sense of dread. Holidays were the worst. It felt like everyone else had a family to go to, and I spent many times sitting alone thinking about the good times others must be having. One of the ways I coped was getting into drugs and alcohol. It gave me an excuse to reject my family. If I could convince myself that it was my choice not to be involved with my family, then at least I could avoid the feeling of being unwanted. But that could only take me so far. Deep down those feelings of rejection and worthlessness festered. It took faith in Jesus and a lot of time for those things to heal.

Perhaps much of that suffering could have been avoided if my parents could have kept their marriage together. I don't hold anything against them for how things happened. I'm just using this as an illustration of why divorce is so damaging, and that is just from the child's perspective. It is also extremely damaging to the couple themselves. Many people feel betrayed. They end up having trust issues for years because the person who promised to love them for the rest of their life leaves them. If divorce happens when someone is older, it can be difficult to find anyone else at a later stage in life. Divorce often involves arguing and turmoil, which causes untold amounts of stress. It can cause difficulties in other relationships too, such as when the couple getting divorced shares the same friend groups. Divorce also often drags on for years and costs thousands of dollars. Some may wonder why anyone would get married at all. But again, the problem isn't due to marriage. It's due to a denigrated view of marriage. Marriage is still a beautiful thing. If you avoid it altogether, you are likely going to miss out on a wonderful part of life. People should try to avoid divorce at all costs, but that doesn't mean they have to avoid marriage too. It just has to be approached in the right way. That's why cohabitation is not a good idea, and why I'm sharing a lot of the lessons I've learned in this book. Creating strong families that stick together will bring about a brighter future for the next generations, and it will make life more fulfilling.

CHAPTER 45

SOCIAL MEDIA

We've covered a lot of ground so far, mostly about how to have a better social life. With that in mind, it would be naive to leave out social media and internet use. These are such a massive part of our society today, and play a huge role in social interaction. Let me kick things off with a section from my senior paper in college that I wrote on Problematic Internet Use:

"There are many possible predictors of Problematic Internet Use that have been proposed such as shyness, loneliness, and social anxiety. (Caplan, 2007; Ceyhan & Ceyhan, 2008; Chak & Leung, 2004; Larose, Lin & Eastin, 2003; Oktan, 2011) These predictors all seem to have some connection with avoiding social interaction. A lack of social skills, a fear of social interaction, or simply a distaste for social interaction in the first place could cause people to seek out the Internet as an escape from real life interactions. The other possibility is that Internet abuse causes people to rely less on their social skills, therefore causing them social anxiety when faced with real interactions. It is likely that Internet Addiction Disorder is a two-way street where certain factors are predictors and also results of excessive Internet use. We need to better understand how the interactions between social skills and Internet use work. It could provide a place for people to go if they dislike social interaction. However, if it is causing social anxiety or diminishing social skills for anyone, these effects could create serious problems for those individuals."[29]

What I'm about to say about social media might cause you to get defensive. I'm going to propose something so radical that you might think I'm a total idiot. You might think that I'm asking way too much from you. You might think that it is totally impossible. Regardless, I'm going to propose it. Get rid of social media! Yes, that's correct. Delete it and don't look back. Are you feeling a little bit defensive yet? That's ok. I understand that social media has been so integrated into society that it seems impossible to leave it behind. Yet, I'm going to say it one more time. Get rid of social media!

You might have thought of a hundred excuses already. "I can keep up with my family." "It's what all my friends do." "I wouldn't have a social life if I deleted social media." "I'll miss out on things." "People will think I'm a weirdo." Whatever the excuses are, I'm going to suggest that they are probably lies or probably irrelevant. I will concede that there can be benefits to social media. However, whatever benefits exist are absolutely miniscule compared to the dangers and downsides. On the other hand, the benefits to deleting your social media accounts are innumerable. It could actually save your life...at least your social life! I know that sounds counterintuitive, but relationships are developed in real life. We need social interaction that happens in actual reality, not just virtual reality. Again, it is possible to have some level of communication online. However, it will always be limited. It will never give you the deep connections you desire and require.

Even science is showing this. The more time people spend on social media, the higher the rates of depression and anxiety.[30] Think about that. Right off the bat, you know that you will be happier if you don't use social media.

So far in this book, we have talked a lot about being authentic and how important that is to developing good relationships. Being authentic on social media is near impossible. People aren't getting to know the real you. They are getting an artificial version of you that you have put forward. Instead of using your body to communicate who you are, you are trying to use a machine.

At the same time, you are not getting to know anyone else authentically. You are seeing a bunch of other people's highlight reels. This constant comparison that happens on social media is only going to make you feel worse. It is going to cause you to lose touch with the true identity you have as a beloved child of

God with unique gifts and talents to offer the world. Instead of seeing yourself in the truth, you are going to think that you are unworthy and unloved. Ironically, one of the reasons you might be going to social media in the first place is to receive validation. You can get likes and followers there. But again, it is artificial and empty. You are only getting likes and followers for the shadow of yourself you have presented. It is never going to fulfill you.

What you are looking for doesn't exist on social media. That is the key truth that has helped me get rid of it. Every time I was about to log on to one of my social media accounts, I reminded myself that I wasn't going to find what I was looking for there. We all have a natural desire to have relationships with people. God designed us that way. We want to love and to be loved, and those are great things, but you will never find them online. Be truly honest with yourself.

Just think about it. Would you rather have a mate that is online or with you in-person? Would you rather hang out in a chat room or chat in a room with real people? Some of you might be thinking that you would prefer the virtual versions, but that is probably because you haven't learned the skills to relate to people in real life very well yet. If you knew that people were going to accept you and love you in real life, would you still prefer the virtual options? The very fact that you are reading this suggests that you would prefer to have great relationships in real life. Is it possible to start a relationship online that ends up being an in-person one also? Yes, but this is not efficient. It's like wanting to get really good at basketball by watching basketball games on TV. You might learn a couple of things about the game, but the way you actually get good is by getting out on the court and shooting free-throws. It's the same with relationships. Why waste your time hoping to develop relationships online when you can be out with real people, learning how to interact with them face to face? That is where you are really going to grow. It probably isn't as comfortable. You will actually have to take some risks and step out of your comfort zone, but it will be effective. In-person is where the growth happens. It's where the breakthroughs happen. It's also where you are going to find fulfillment in your relationships. You won't find that online.

Getting off social media isn't going to be easy. At first it will probably be painful. You will literally have to go through withdrawals. Social media sites are designed to give you the same dopamine hits that drugs like cocaine and heroin give people. They can literally turn your brain into that of an addict's. You will also probably have fear of missing out. Yes, you may actually miss out on some things. However, these things are trivial and not worth your time. Just accept that missing out on some things is part of the cost. What you are giving up pales in comparison to what you will gain. Once you have gotten over your fears, you won't even care about missing things because you will enjoy the things that happen in real life so much more.

Let me give you an example. When I was on social media, I spent hours every day looking at what people I knew were doing in their lives, I argued with people over political and social issues, and I posted personal stories because I wanted to connect with people I could share my life with. The thing is, all of those activities, all of those hours spent browsing social media, rarely led to any kind of deep personal connection with anyone. Occasionally, I might connect with an old friend or learn about an in-person event that was happening, but those occasions were rare. The return on my investment of time was insanely disproportional. On top of that, many of the arguments I got into actually hurt my relationships. I actually lost connection with friends and family members, simply because we got in a comment argument on facebook, and couldn't resolve it easily the way we would have normally been able to in person.

When I finally decided to leave these social media platforms behind, it was difficult, but well worth it. I thought I would be missing out on all kinds of opportunities. I thought it would be hard to keep in touch with friends. Sure, there are things I missed out on, and still miss out on. However, what I found was so much richer. The friends I had in real life became a much higher priority in my life. I was forced to reach out to people in person. I started having deep conversations with people, and I found that I was able to share what was on my heart and mind so much more efficiently and effectively. I found myself noticing what was happening in the present more often. My anxiety levels plummeted. I realized that the things I was missing out on weren't that important. If they would have been, I would have put in the energy to experience them outside of social media, which is what I started doing with things that actually were important to me. My life became more real. It was more tangible and solid. Leaving social media freed up my mind to focus on what was happening right in front of me rather than paying attention to all these different esoteric things that were happening online. Giving up social media was a huge positive for me. On top of that, if you get even a little bit skilled at interacting with people in real life, you will seem like a social rockstar because so many people are totally incompetent in this area nowadays. You don't have to do much to stand out in a crowd of people who have been conditioned to living on the internet.

Try it out for yourself. You can always go back to using social media if you find that leaving is somehow detrimental to your life. There is literally zero risk in trying it out for a little while. As you begin, you might face some pressure from people not to do it. Hold out and maintain your position. Stay strong for at least a month. People will likely come around, and may even start looking up to you as a leader. Perhaps others will see how much better your life is and want to join you. And look, I get it. If you have social media under control and only use it for business or contacting your grandma, you probably don't need to delete it. This isn't law. I still have YouTube for learning things and sharing my creative projects. However, from what I've seen and heard, most people don't have social media under control. It rules their lives, wasting their time and causing them to be depressed and anxious. If that's the case for you, what I'm suggesting isn't that radical. It might give you a freedom you didn't even realize existed.

CHAPTER 46

ANTISOCIAL SKILLS

Now we are going to shift gears a bit. Not all the pitfalls to watch out for are big controversial topics. There are some basic social behaviors that could trip you up as well. This section is kind of like the corollary to the social skills portion of this book. Rather than explaining how to do things that will positively affect your relationships, this section contains a bunch of the things you want to avoid doing. I will call them antisocial skills. This is not to be confused with the clinical usage of the term such as in antisocial personality disorder. It is just meant to be a way of describing how these behaviors are diametrically opposed to good social skills.

These things can be trickier than you might think. Some will seem like obviously stupid things to do, but others will actually seem very practical. Some may even be effective, at least in the short term. However, they will all inevitably lead to dysfunction. Imagine a con artist who is able to deceive his victim into believing he is genuine. There are things he does that actually work to produce a positive reaction in others, but you can also see that his relationships are shallow and dysfunctional. Someone looking from the outside would not consider any of the victims as the con man's friends. They can see that he is putting on a mask in order to deceive them. Inevitably, the victim will realize the con man was fake all along and the relationship will fall apart, either because they sense that he is fake or because they get seriously hurt. That's not what I desire for you. I am trying to equip you to have good, healthy relationships.

Some of the other behaviors I'll cover here are little things that may cause people to find you annoying or simply reduce your results. Again, this isn't about trying to be perfect. Acting like that is actually one of the things that will make people dislike you. This is about helping you to be aware of the behaviors you might be doing that are pushing people away.

So with that, I will hop into the one I just mentioned, acting like you are perfect. Really, this is just another description for pride. It could be stated in other ways as well, such as thinking you are better than or above other people, acting condescending, minimizing your failures and shortcomings, being cocky or arrogant, and many others. They all stem from the same root of pride.

This is tricky because confidence and pride can seem similar on the surface, but one will help you while the other will destroy you. Confidence comes from being secure in your identity, while pride actually comes from being insecure. When people desire to be confident, but aren't grounded in their identity, they can try to project that confidence through their outward behaviors. That's why pride is boastful and arrogant. Instead of acting from a true place of confidence, pride tries to display confidence outwardly in hopes that others will perceive this as true confidence.

Sometimes it works, at least temporarily, but most people can pick up on it pretty quickly. If they do, they aren't going to like it. Pride makes others feel small. Since a person acting out of pride doesn't have true strength, they have to put others down to make themselves feel like they are strong enough. A person who is prideful will be reluctant to admit their mistakes because they are afraid that they aren't strong enough to bear the consequences. This makes it very hard to work through problems in a relationship with them because if there is a rupture in the relationship it requires the admission of guilt and sorrow for hurting the other person. Without that, forgiveness is difficult and the restoration of the relationship is near impossible. Even if a person would choose to continue that kind of relationship, there will always be some underlying resentment.

Acting prideful will also cause people to work against you. Pride is confrontational and selfish. People who act pridefully interact with people from a competitive stance rather than a cooperative one. This automatically puts people in opposition to them. Prideful people also inspire a sense of fear. If others seem like they like them, it is often because they fear them.

Pride is something you definitely want to avoid. The opposite of pride is humility, which is a tremendous trait to help your relationships. It doesn't mean becoming weak or looking down on yourself. True humility comes from a place of strength. You don't have to prove anything to anyone because you are confident in your identity. Humility puts the good of others above oneself. It seeks to help and uplift others. In turn, they will often uplift and help you. Strive for humility in your relationships and avoid pride.

I've already talked about how telling the truth will benefit you. Now I'm going to talk about dishonesty, and how it can be a major antisocial skill. Dishonesty is tricky because it isn't always the direct opposite of the truth. More often than not it contains some truth with lies mixed in. It could also include purposely concealing the truth without deliberately lying. Dishonesty can be an easy trap to fall into.

Lies are often used as a way of protecting oneself, but it is a dysfunctional and fragile form of protection. It usually doesn't last and it comes with consequences. Think about a bluff in poker vs actually having a royal flush. The bluff will only work if the other person buys into it. If they decide to call you on it, you lose everything. Whereas if you actually have a royal flush, you can be confident that you are going to win. You are holding on to something solid and tangible.

By now you should know that authenticity, vulnerability, and trust are key for building strong healthy relationships. Dishonesty kills all of those things. Even if you get away with dishonesty, there are going to be other consequences.

For example, you aren't going to have confidence in yourself because you will know it is based on a lie. You will also have to remember your lies if anyone asks you about them, which will take up mental capital. There are a bunch of awful things that come from dishonesty. For the purpose of this section, it will cause people to distrust you, which will keep them far away. No one wants to be around someone they can't trust. It's actually dangerous for them. Being dishonest is a guaranteed way of ruining your relationships.

An antisocial behavior related to dishonesty is playing games with people. This is a form of dishonesty that purposely uses manipulation in order to get a desired reaction out of someone. This is an extremely dangerous trap to fall into because it can easily be justified by saying things like, "This is just how the world works." For example, I have met women who keep men around as friends in case things don't work out with their current mate. Some even do it just to get attention from these other men, purposely making them believe she is interested in them romantically, while never intending anything in that regard. I've seen men do things like purposely get a woman super excited to go on a date and then cancel at the last minute using a fake excuse in order to create a strong emotional reaction in the woman. If you end up in a relationship with someone like this, it is more than likely not going to end well. Again, this is why honesty and authenticity are so important. Without them, someone always gets hurt. This doesn't mean you will always be able to be perfectly honest or that if you accidentally lie to someone that you are a horrible manipulator. Just do your best. If your intention is to be honest, that is enough.

For the next social pitfall I will start with an example. I had a friend back in highschool who I respected in a lot of ways, but there was one behavior he did that drove me nuts. Whenever someone told a story, he would always try to one up them. If they told a story about bench pressing 225 lbs, he would tell the story of when he benched 250 lbs. If they told a story about some cool trick their dog did, he would tell a story about an even cooler trick his dog did. Once in a while, it is ok to tell a similar story to someone in order to try to relate to them, and I honestly think that is at least part of what my friend was trying to do. He just failed to notice how it was actually coming across.

When people tell stories, they often want to feel like you heard them. They want to bring you into their experience. Stories often have a deep personal significance for the person. If you instantly one up them, they are going to feel like their story is insignificant and that they now have to compete with you. It's usually not going to cause people to like you. It can easily come off as arrogant.

If you really want to tell a similar story, at least make sure you acknowledge the other person's story first. Express how it made you feel. Try to compliment them on some aspect of it. Repeat it back in your own words, or at least part of it, so the other person knows you heard and understood them. Once they are totally finished, then you can share your story. Just be very careful not to minimize what the other person shared while simultaneously bragging about yourself.

Another approach that could actually get a laugh is by telling a story that is absurdly *less* interesting than the other person's story. For example, if the person told you about a vacation they took to an exotic country, you could say something like, "I once took a road trip all the way to the other side of town." As I said, this will probably get a laugh because it's not what people are expecting, and it will make the other person feel good about getting to take their trip to an exotic country. It is great to learn how to tell stories and you should endeavor to do it more often. Just be careful you aren't using them to one up other people.

Another behavior to avoid is always relying on other people to start conversations. As I've noted earlier, it is good to allow silence and space, and you don't want to totally dominate an interaction. However, that is not what I'm talking about here. This is more about not being a boring person. If you never have anything to say, people are going to lose interest in being around you. Allow yourself to speak whatever you're thinking. Try to come up with interesting questions to ask people. This doesn't mean you have to talk about things you don't care about. Rather, find what you're passionate about and then talk about those things. It could be totally nerdy. I often find myself in conversations about Lord of the Rings or astronomy. If you are passionate about it, people will be interested. This will help them get to know you.

A pitfall related to always relying on others for conversation is answering questions with simple answers. This is a sure fire way to kill a conversation. For example, if someone asks you where you are from, you could tell them the city you live in with a one word answer, or you could share a story about how you got there. You want to give the person something to latch onto. Compare these two different replies. "Where are you from?" "Minnesota." "Where are you from?" "I just moved back to Minnesota after traveling around the country as a missionary." The second one gives someone way more to work with than the simple one-word response. Maybe they enjoy traveling and you can then pivot and talk about that, or maybe they were in mission work or just moved to Minnesota too. You are giving the other person a few different options for relating to you. You are giving them choices for conversational threads you can go deeper into. If I just say, "Minnesota," that doesn't tell the person much about me and it brings the conversation to a sudden halt. Try to be a little more deliberate about answering questions. It's a conversation not an interrogation.

I've already discussed active listening earlier in the book, but this is a good time to mention some behaviors that will inhibit your ability to listen. Since I just talked about giving good answers to questions, I'll give a caveat to that. Don't try to think of your answers while another person is speaking. Listening requires your full attention. If you are trying to come up with a perfect answer before letting the other person finish, you are going to miss out on what they say. Wait until they are finished, and then formulate your answer. This will ensure you get all the information first, and it will allow you to think without any distractions. It's ok to pause and sit in silence for a minute if you need to think deeply. This is much less awkward than realizing you didn't hear what the other person said. If you need time, try to relate what the other person said back to them in your own words and see if they agree. The point is that you want to do your best to listen to them.

Another behavior that will inhibit your ability to listen is being on your phone. This can be a major distraction in conversations. You should set a goal for yourself to never even look at your phone if you are in a conversation with someone. Not only will it cause you to miss what they are saying, but it is a visible sign you aren't listening and the person who is speaking will see that. A person can feel extremely disrespected if someone is on their phone while the person is trying to talk to them. There are obviously exceptions in emergency situations, but try to avoid them unless it's absolutely necessary. If you are expecting an important call or text message, tell the person you are talking to ahead of time. Let them know you might have to interrupt the conversation to check your phone. Even if you aren't in a serious conversation, I would suggest staying off your phone anytime you are with people. Relationships are about being present. Why focus your attention on distant virtual relationships while you are with people in real life? Keeping your phone put away while you are with people is a simple habit that can create a massive change.

The conversational pitfall I'll mention next is being outright disrespectful. Try to be kind to people. That doesn't mean you let people walk all over you. It's important to maintain boundaries and stand up for what is right. But even in the most tense situation imaginable there is almost always a way to do that respectfully. It's not always easy. People will push your buttons sometimes. Still, try to respond with respect. It will help you maintain your dignity, and oftentimes it can be the greatest comeback. It displays patience and humility. Those are qualities people like to be around.

One fatal mistake you can make in relationships is moving too quickly. I will try to clarify what I mean by that because it is a very specific type of behavior I'm talking about. By moving too quickly I mean giving too much of yourself away without getting anything in return. This could be giving away your attention, your time, your money, or your body. It doesn't mean relationships are transactional, and it doesn't mean that you should move quickly if the other person *does* reciprocate. What I'm trying to say is that when you throw yourself at someone too strongly, it is likely going to push them away.

Imagine you are standing next to your own brand new Ferrari and someone compliments you on it. Would you respond by giving them the spare set of keys? No way! You might offer them a ride, but you aren't going to entrust them with the keys. It's the same with relationships. You don't want to invest every part of yourself right off the bat. Imagine another scenario. You go on a first date with someone that goes pretty well. You seem to have a connection and would be open to going on another date. Then the next morning you get a text from them that says, "I had so much fun last night. I want to be with you forever. I will never leave you no matter what." I hope that would raise some huge red flags. Personally, I would be running for the hills. If someone is willing to compromise on anything to be with you, it signals that they probably have low standards and weak morals. Yet, it is easy to fall into this trap. When you really like someone, you can begin to imagine what they might be like, and that begins to create this sort of infatuation for the person. These imaginings are a distortion of reality. It is much better to learn about who people actually are. That takes time.

Allow people to discover who you are slowly. Reveal things as it is natural to reveal them. This creates opportunities for people to be pleasantly surprised. For example, many people don't know that I play the harmonica. When I pull it out and start riffing, they really enjoy it because it was a talent of mine they didn't realize I had. The point here isn't to purposely hold yourself back, though you may need to be intentional if you really struggle with giving too much away too quickly. The goal should be to let things unfold organically. Be present in the moment. Set some standards and wait for other people to meet them. I do want to point out the danger of taking it too far the other way. You can also begin to set your standards too high, which will lead to frustration when no one lives up to them. That is why it is important to work on yourself too. Don't hold anyone to standards that you don't maintain yourself.

There you have it. Those are some of the most common traps when it comes to social skills. There are likely many more as well, but these are the ones I could think of. After you begin to socialize with people more, you should be able to intuitively pick up on what works and what doesn't. With some experience it should become common sense. Eventually, you will just know that something is hurting you socially. You will be able to feel it.

You can probably already feel it in extreme situations. It's those behaviors that make you cringe. It's that feeling you get when you're watching a movie and want to shout, "What are you doing!? You idiot!" at the characters on screen. It's ok if things are a little awkward from time to time, especially if you are new to this. Just try to avoid things that make people actively avoid you. If you implement what you've learned in this book so far, you should do just fine.

CHAPTER 47

CONFIRMATION BIAS

A pitfall big enough to merit its own chapter is confirmation bias. Confirmation bias is the idea that a person will make choices that confirm their deeply held beliefs, and avoid situations that challenge them. As people learn about how the world works, they can begin to make broad assumptions that aren't necessarily true. For example, I have heard some men say that all women are lying, manipulative, cheaters who will leave a man as soon as they find someone better. I actually held that belief myself at one point. There are certainly examples of that happening, and if you are a man you should try to avoid those types of women. However, when a person speaks in broad generalizations like that as if it were settled truth, they can then fall into confirmation bias.

This is a problem for multiple reasons. I stated that

confirmation bias is the idea that people will make choices that confirm their beliefs. What kind of women do you think men who believe that all women are lying cheaters will end up with? If there is confirmation bias, it will likely be lying and cheating women. That isn't because they are the only types of women that exist. It is because the man is actively looking for women that confirm his belief. To a man with confirmation bias, it is more painful to admit he is wrong than to end up with a lying and cheating woman. It only gets worse from there. Ending up with a lying cheating woman only further confirms the bias in the man's mind. If a good trustworthy woman comes along, the man will find a way to sabotage any chance of a relationship with her because it would mean letting go of his belief. Confirmation bias acts like a defense mechanism in this case. It comes from a place of fear. Admitting that there are good trustworthy women would mean the man has to relinquish his control and make himself vulnerable, but that is the only way for him to have a good healthy relationship. Confirmation bias is often used as a way to avoid something. Maybe it's rejection. Maybe it's conflict. Whatever the case, it is good to be aware of it because if you can spot it, you can change it.

A good way to do this is to try to figure out what your most deeply held beliefs are, and then challenge them. This doesn't mean that you can't have beliefs or that beliefs aren't good. There are many things that are true, and you should defend them. However, if something is actually true, it will hold up to scrutiny. Try to think of any examples that would counter your belief. This is how science works.

Let me give you an example of how to fix confirmation bias. If you hold the belief that you always quit things before they are finished, try to find examples of things you *have* finished. If you can find them, then that belief isn't an absolute truth. That's important because if you hold the belief that not finishing things is who you are and there is no changing it, there is a high probability that you will self-sabotage every time you are close to finishing something. Rather than challenging your belief, you will seek to confirm it. However, if you can think of examples of finishing things you started, that can be motivation to finish whatever it is you are presently working on. If there is a different belief that you want to change, simply apply the same process.

Confirmation bias can make figuring out what you believe difficult. If it is strong enough, it can cause a person to avoid seeing what their false beliefs are altogether. Journaling can be a great way to figure out what those hidden beliefs are. Asking friends to help can be a good idea too. Sometimes other people can see what we ourselves can't. Figuring out these biases and rooting them out can make a big difference in your relationships and your life. It's well worth paying attention to. In the context of relationships, deeply held beliefs can be the very thing holding us back, and changing those beliefs can create the biggest changes in our social lives.

CONCLUSION

We've covered a lot of material on relationships and social interaction in this book. Let's review briefly. First, I wrote about why relationships are important. We are literally wired for them. There is a lack of meaning and depth without other people to share life with. I then addressed some of the reasons we might have problems with relationships. Many of us didn't have good role models or instruction on what healthy relationships look like. Once we got an understanding of the issue, we dove into how to improve things. It begins with being secure in your identity. My most repeated statement was something like, "You are a unique person created in the image of God with dignity and value." Until you know that in the depths of your being you won't be able to have high quality relationships. Then I gave you some ways to grow in confidence including healing from trauma, finding mentors and friends, and drawing good boundaries. I wrote about masculinity and femininity, and how they complement each other. I wrote about character building and virtue. I wrote about God and His role in our lives. Basically, there was a lot of info on how to become a strong and confident individual who feels fulfilled in life. From there, we pivoted towards the social skills aspect of things. This was the section about what behaviors to start incorporating in your social interactions to make them go better. There was a huge variety of things from body language to what kind of attitude to have. Finally, we ended with what to avoid. This was probably the most controversial part of the book, but included some extremely important discussions about things that can greatly affect relationships.

The info contained in this book is by no means comprehensive. I could have continued writing and writing, adding more and more topics, and I actually did that quite a bit anyways. Human relationships are complicated. There are a lot of aspects to consider. People study these things for years trying to understand them. Hopefully, this will at least give you a solid foundation to begin and to build. You don't need to know every intricacy of facial expression in order to hold a conversation with someone. You don't need to know the precise neural paths that neurotransmitters take when people bond with each other to be able to build healthy relationships. Knowing some basic fundamentals will be plenty for most people.

If you apply what's in this book, I'm confident you will see improvements in your social life, and hopefully life in general. If you haven't started, now is the time to act. Put the concepts found in this book to use and see what happens. If you encounter a specific problem, I encourage you to go back and look for a solution based on whatever it is. You are going to get the most out of this book if you use it like a toolbox. When you are noticing a problem area, pull out the right tool to fix it. I truly hope this book is a blessing for you, and that through improved relationships, your entire life will flourish.

If you found the information in this book valuable, please check out **www.movingamountain.com/books** where you can download a free e-book version of the book that can easily be shared with others.

I made the electronic version of this book available for free because I want anyone to be able to access it. If you want to read it, you should be able to. I poured my heart and soul into writing it because I desire people to have successful relationships and satisfying social lives. There seemed to be a gap that needed to be filled in this area, and I believe this information can help. If you understand the importance of that, please share it with others. Thank you so much for your support. Maranatha!

For public speaking inquiries, visit **www.movingamountain.com/speaking**

Notes

1. Scheremet, William. "The Effect of Problematic Internet Use on Social and Psychological Well Being." University of Minnesota. 2012.

2. Pew Research Center. "Teens, Social Media and Technology 2018." May 31, 2018. https://www.pewresearch.org/internet/2018/05/31/teens-social-media-technology-2018/.

3. Centre for Addiction and Mental Health. "Social media use and mental health among students in Ontario." *CAMH Population Studies eBulletin* 19, no. 2 (September 2018). https://www.camh.ca/-/media/files/pdfs---ebulletin/ebulletin-19-n2-socialmedia-mental-health-2017osduhs-pdf.pdf.

4. Young, K.S. "Internet addiction: The emergence of a new clinical disorder." *CyberPsychology & Behavior* 1, no. 3 (1998): 237-244.

5. Raquel Kennedy Bergen and Kathleen A. Bogle. "Exploring the Connection Between Pornography and Sexual Violence." Violence and Victims 15, no. 3 (Fall 2000): 227-234. https://www.ojp.gov/ncjrs/virtual-library/abstracts/exploring-connection-between-pornography-and-sexual-violence.

6. Brown, Susan L. "Marriage and Child Well-Being: Research and Policy Perspectives." *Journal of Marriage and Family* 72, no. 5 (October 2010): 1059-1077. https://www.ncbi.nlm.nih.gov/pmc/articles/PMC3091824/.

7. Watson, Stephanie. "Oxytocin: The love hormone." Harvard Health Publishing. July 20, 2021. https://www.health.harvard.edu/mind-and-mood/oxytocin-the-love-hormone.

8. Farquhar, Brodie. "Wolf Reintroduction Changes Ecosystem in Yellowstone." Yellowstone National Park Trips. June 30, 2021. https://www.yellowstonepark.com/things-to-do/wildlife/wolf-reintroduction-changes-ecosystem/.

9. Ackerman, Courtney E. "What is Attachment Theory? Bowlby's 4 Stages Explained." Positive Psychology. April 27, 2018. https://positivepsychology.com/attachment-theory/.

10. Rebecca A. Williamson, Vikram K. Jaswal, and Andrew N. Meltzoff. "Learning the Rules: Observation and Imitation of a Sorting Strategy by 36-Month-Old Children." *Developmental Psychology* 46, no. 1 (January 2010): 57-65. https://www.ncbi.nlm.nih.gov/pmc/articles/PMC3116636/.

11. "Good Sleep for Good Health." *NIH News in Health* (April 2021): 1-2. https://newsinhealth.nih.gov/sites/nih-NIH/files/2021/April/NIHNiHApr2021.pdf.

12. Westley, Rosa. "Sleep Patterns – A Simple Explanation Of Your Four Nightly Sleep Cycles." Sleep Authority. September 22, 2018. https://www.sleepauthority.com/how-sleep-works/sleep-patterns/.

13. Takahiko Koike, Motofumi Sumiya, Eri Nakagawa, Shuntaro Okazaki and Norihiro Sadato. "What Makes Eye Contact Special? Neural Substrates of On-Line Mutual Eye-Gaze: A Hyperscanning fMRI Study." *eNeuro* 6, no. 1 (January 2019) https://www.eneuro.org/content/6/1/ENEURO.0284-18.2019.

14. Lehman, Karl. "Regaining Access-Humor." In *Outsmarting Yourself: Catching Your Past Invading the Present and What to Do About It,* 215-218. Liberty, Illinois: This JOY! Books, 2011.

15. Donald L. Hilton, Jr and Clark Watts. "Pornography addiction: A neuroscience perspective." *Surgical Neurology International* 2, no. 19 (February 2011) https://www.ncbi.nlm.nih.gov/pmc/articles/PMC3050060/.

16. Todd Love, Christian Laier, Matthias Brand, Linda Hatch, and Raju Hajela. "Neuroscience of Internet Pornography Addiction: A Review and Update." *Behavioral Sciences* 5, no. 3 (September 2015): 388-433. https://www.ncbi.nlm.nih.gov/pmc/articles/PMC4600144/.

17. Kleinman, Alexis. "Porn Sites Get More Visitors Each Month Than Netflix, Amazon And Twitter Combined." Huffpost. December 6, 2017. https://www.huffpost.com/entry/internet-porn-stats_n_3187682.

18. Pew Research Center. "America's Abortion Quandary." May 6, 2022. https://www.pewresearch.org/religion/2022/05/06/americas-abortion-quandary/.

19. Health Research Funding. "18 Shocking Statistics Abortion Rape Victims." Accessed January 22, 2023. https://healthresearchfunding.org/18-shocking-abortion-statistics-rape-victims/

20. Frankl, Viktor. *Man's Search for Meaning.* Austria: Beacon Press, 1946.

21. Centers for Disease Control and Prevention. "Suicide Data and Statistics." Accessed November 20, 2022. https://www.cdc.gov/suicide/suicide-data-statistics.html.

22. Clowes, Brian. "The Strange World of Margaret Sanger's Birth Control Review: Part II." Human Life International. April 18, 2017. https://www.hli.org/resources/sangers-birth-control-review-part-ii/.

23. Johnston, Robert. "United States abortion rates, 1960-2013." Last modified November 28, 2014. http://www.johnstonsarchive.net/policy/abortion/graphusabrate.html.

24. Taylor, Kathleen. "How Birth Control Messes Up Mutual Attraction." Natural Womanhood. December 10, 2020. https://naturalwomanhood.org/how-the-birth-control-pill-messes-up-mutual-attraction/.

25. Smith, Janet. "Contraception: Why Not?" Catholic Education Resource Center. August 2005. https://www.catholiceducation.org/en/controversy/common-misconceptions/contraception-why-not.html.

26. Meads, Tim. "Transgender Inmate Impregnates Two Female Prisoners At New Jersey's Women Only Prison, Report Says." The Daily Wire. April 14, 2022. https://www.dailywire.com/news/transgender-inmate-impregnates-two-female-prisoners-at-new-jerseys-women-only-prison-report-says.

27. Michael J. Rosenfeld and Katharina Roesler. "Cohabitation Experience and Cohabitation's Association With Marital Dissolution." *Journal of Marriage and Family* 81, no. 1 (September 2018): 42-58. https://onlinelibrary.wiley.com/doi/10.1111/jomf.12530.

28. Regnerus, Mark. "How different are the adult children of parents who have same-sex relationships? Findings from the New Family Structures Study." *Social Science Research* 41, no. 4 (July 2012): 752-770. https://www.sciencedirect.com/science/article/abs/pii/S0049089X12000610.

29. Scheremet, "The Effect of Problematic Internet Use on Social and Psychological Well Being."

30. Ariel Shensa, Jaime E. Sidani, Mary Amanda Dew, César G. Escobar-Viera, and Brian A. Primack. "Social Media Use and Depression and Anxiety Symptoms: A Cluster Analysis." *American Journal of Health Behavior* 42, no. 2 (March 2018): 116-128. https://www.ncbi.nlm.nih.gov/pmc/articles/PMC5904786/.

Author Bio

William Scheremet was a drug addicted, thrill seeking, hedonist for most of his teens and early 20s. After breaking his back in a motocross accident and coming to know Jesus Christ, his life changed dramatically. Now William seeks to live his life for God and for others, and enjoys much greater happiness and fulfillment. He shares his newfound perspective through writing, filmmaking, music, and other ventures.

www.ingramcontent.com/pod-product-compliance
Lightning Source LLC
Chambersburg PA
CBHW051141130726
47988CB00005B/1938